God's Goal in Creation

God's Goal
In Creation

Gaining a Fresh Perspective
on Evil & The Purposes of God

τελος

PUBLICATIONS

iv

DEDICATION

To all those—from as far back as my conversion from a strongly atheistic world view in 1976—who have helped me in my walk of faith, and to those who have both aided and encouraged me in my interest and 'quest' in the apologetic task—especially regarding the 'Problem of Evil'. Thank You.

A Big 'Thank You' to Professor Christopher Southgate. Chris was my main supervisor (2011-2015) whilst undertaking postgraduate research at the University of Exeter. Chris may not have, totally, persuaded me with his arguments but his advice and guidance have been immeasurably beneficial. Last but not least: a special thank you to my wife of fifty six years, Jackie, who is, by now, used to my long absences—away with the note pads, books and Lap Top—occasionally construed as 'Derek's excuse to avoid gardening or decorating.

A considerable part of this book (excluding the numerous changes and additions—and there have been many) is taken from the Master of Research Degree Thesis (2015) awarded by the University of Exeter.

CONTENTS

Preface   (Page 9)

Introduction   (Page 24)

Part1: GOOD

Four Letter Words   (Page 36)

No other 'Good'   (Page 39)

Constraints on God   (Page 41)

Questions of Ontological Veracity (Page 43)

Process Thought and Omnipotence (Page 50)

Goodness in the Hebrew Scriptures   (Page 55)

'Goodness' in Question   (Page 61)

Part2: Differing Perspectives

'Red in Tooth & Claw'   (Page 65)

Blaming a 'lesser deity' (Page 69)

End Time Answers: Waiting for the Parousia (Page 73)

Obscuring Beginnings: Karl Barth & Nature   (Page 80)

Against Instrumentalism: 'Cause & Effect'   (Page 88)

Irenaeus & Augustine: Differing Perspectives   (Page 93)

Evolution: God's Response to Rebellion   (99)

Beyond 'pure' Darwinism   (Page 104)

Part3: Regarding Extra-terrestrials

'Made a Little Lower than the Angels'   (Page 114)

Ape-Men & Angels   (Page 120)

'In the Beginning' Angels   (Page 142)

Angels and Free-Will   (Page 149)

Free Will, Angels and Sovereignty   (Page 153)

Angels with Intent   (Page 158)

Rationale for the Angelic Fall   (Page 161)

Biospheric Consequences   (Page 169)

Post Fall Subjugation   (Page 175)

Part4: God is Still Good

Beauty & The Beast   (Page 184)

An 'evolutionary devil' in The Detail   (Page 192)

Creaturely Flourishing   (Page 208)

Is Heaven a Necessary 'World'?   (Page 212)

Part5: TELOS

Only Such a World   (Page 223)

The Goal of Creation   (Page 234)

The Justice of God   (Page 238)

Beyond Mere-Metaphysics   (Page 239)

Events Have Consequences   (Page 244)

The Future, Our Future   (Page 251)

Summary   (Page 255)

Appendix   (Page 267) "Thinking 'Allowed' on World Views"

PREFACE

During a radio interview,[1] a well-known naturalist [WKN] gave a hasty corrective when the interviewer described him as an atheist. The dialogue went something like this: [WKN] " No, I am not an atheist, I'm an agnostic (or words to that effect) ." [Interviewer] " So you believe that God 'set up' the system of nature?" [WKN] "No, I do not, but I sometimes think [e.g. while observing a termite's hill], that there is an unobserved observer." WKN's take on 'god' would, in my opinion, fall into the category of both an impotent and disinterested 'deity. If the Judeo Christian God is a deity who likes to observe his handiwork but has no intention of interfering with or intervening in his world, however 'messed up' it may be, we had best forget the whole notion of a personal God and make the most of life without his personal intervention, attention or care.

Evil and the Goodness of God is such a 'big' subject, a subject that fills the shelves of libraries; indeed, many have devoted their lives to attempting to resolve it.

---

[1] Radio 4 Saturday January 31st 2009

The question of, how an alleged God of Love, who is 'All Powerful', can allow such evil to continue to exist is one that will not go away. But why is it that we humans have the temerity to demand an explanation from God or to doubt the existence of the God of the Bible because we find [this particular] God under qualified or wanting? Doesn't it strike one as rather odd that the very argument against God's goodness comes from the notion of the actual existence of 'good and evil'—a belief that owes its origins to the Judeo/Christian Scriptures—and a malevolence that has its origins in another source. What guarantee have we that these precious social mores (that we in the 'West' take for granted) do not evaporate 'overnight' under the weight of 'other ideas'— ideas that are socially engineered and not universally absolute? Of course many societies adhere to other ideas—ideas that see 'black as white and white as black'—yet there is a strange notion of injustice at the 'heart'—and that is because of the existence of GOD—The Alpha and Omega: 'who was and is and is to come.' (Revelation 1:8)

If we really believed that 'Natural Selection' was, solely, the prime mover for biological life, we ought not to be asking such a question—though the problem can, to some degree, be lessened if our view of God's involvement in the creative process. God's 'handiwork' is undetectable simply because evolution is a natural process and needs no meddling from 'without'. The undetectability of purpose—or the 'Hand of God' is not evidence for purposelessness as there may well be an 'overall' purpose to biological evolution. Indeed this is the view of the proponents of Theistic Evolution. Indeed, as the biochemist Denis Alexander points out, 'Nomic (law-like) regularity is a consistent feature' and that the 'question of existence' seems to cast doubt on the claim that, 'this whole process is without Purpose.' (2018). The idea that there is a 'big picture'—that God is not the 'God of The Gaps' is fully appreciated, however, it makes it difficult to allow for the existence of the God of Scripture—for the feasibility of actual providence. Should such a God as the God of the Judeo Christian Scriptures exist, we would expect reciprocal moral standards— though; it might be argued that the 'Theistic Evolutionary View' relieves us from that particular conundrum.

It is said that the inherent goodness of God means that God is the final standard of good and that all that God is and does is worthy of approval. i.e. God's approval, not man's! God, therefore, is the final standard of good. If this is the case, then we can say that 'Goodness' emanates from the heart of God. God is 'good' as opposed to 'bad' or even malevolent. Goodness then, both seen and unseen[2], comes from God. The good we experience therefore comes from only one source, God. If God is not good, then we have no reason to put our trust in him (if I may be permitted to use the masculine pronoun)—for he may not be trustworthy.

If we do not trust God, then we cannot say we have faith in God. To say we have faith in someone but do not trust them is akin to the phrase 'the living dead'—it is an oxymoron. Hebrews 11:6 though says that without faith/trust it is not possible to please God.

N.T. Wright (2006) refers to 'the problem of good'. Why he argues, should there be such a thing as good? It is because goodness is the essence of God. This is not to say that we have, what some would describe as 'coherent' answers for many of the big questions about evil and suffering. Presuppositions about evil and God's alleged culpability will always be with us—some will never be satisfied no matter what is said. If God is good, we can trust in his goodness—in his ultimate triumph over all that is perceived to be 'not good'. This is the argument throughout this book.

Why should it be the case that life has value, that suffering matters, that evil is an affront to our standards? If our sense of morality has, somehow, evolved through natural selection, we could expect changes—we would not expect a universal absolute—an absolute that differentiates, reasonably clearly, between 'good and evil—between 'right and wrong'. Indeed suffering does not and cannot matter to a mindless process that 'sees not' and 'cares not' yet 'intervenes', through biological determinism, in order for Natural Selection's 'objective' to prevail, or should we say, 'to continue its program of survival'·

In his provocative and controversial work, The Selfish Gene, Richard Dawkins contends that all human behaviour is based primarily on genetic survival. Dawkins [argues] that genes have a long evolutionary history of survival and they control nearly every aspect of human behaviour. Various proteins evolved and mutated into molecules that copied themselves repeatedly and eventually various strands of DNA developed. The DNA copies itself and determines not only the phenotype (i.e. the organism's physical characteristics) but the behaviour of the organism as well for the sole purpose of survival. The fundamental rule is that the DNA directs all organisms, from amoebas to apes, for the purposes of adaptation, survival and reproduction. "Dawkins advanced the thesis that the genes function as 'replicators'; these replicators' primary task is survival by whatever means necessary. So for Dawkins, individual humans simply function as 'vehicles' for the replicators of survival." [3]

The question of 'right and wrong'—morality seems to be a universal given—inculcated into our very psyche. It is not a natural phenomenon—a by-product of evolutionary biology. We [the human race], instinctively know that 'things' are not the way they should be, we know that the things we do are sometimes an affront to 'the moral code'—whatever that might be…

---

[3] BAD TO THE BONE? ORIGINAL SIN, EVOLUTION AND NATURAL LAW,Craig A. Boyd Dept. of Philosophy Azusa Pacific University.

In countries with, what might be called, 'Christian Heritage ' (such as the UK) our sense of fairness, our 'moral compass' [4] is, mostly, derived from the teachings of The Bible (Old and New Testaments). If this is so, we should expect to see evidence of these values, and we do. The Apostle Paul puts it so succinctly when he says that he tried everything, but nothing helped—that there was nothing 'anybody' could do for him—for us. Then he wrote these words: "The answer, thank God, is that Jesus Christ can and does. He acted to set things right in this life of contradictions where I want to serve God with my heart and mind, but am pulled by the influence of my 'natural inclinations' to do something totally different ." Romans 7:25 (The Message). When we look at the state of things in the world; when we look at the results of both 'moral' and 'natural' evil we may conclude that either God does not abide by 'His' own moral code or that there is another explanation for the pain, suffering and death we see all around us. Some philosophers and apologists refer to a 'greater good'—that somehow all will be made right—that all the BIG questions will have answers—that God will be vindicated because it is God alone who is GOOD.

---

[4] This is an overused/abused expression—used, mainly, by politicians to bring 'comfort' to the distrusting electorate. Nevertheless there is such a beast within us all—a moral compass that, for so many, is but a flickering remnant—the echo of the 'Thou shall nots….."

I maintain that God is GOOD—'The GOOD'. Quite frankly though, I do not have enough knowledge of God's dealings—of 'a future good'—a good that all those who love him will 'see' and all those who are (have been or will be) innocent victims will experience. We may make pronouncements about God's apparent failures—God's lack of 'goodness', but let us do so with the humility of the 'uninformed'. It is, as the apostle Paul says: '……we do not see clearly for our vision is impaired'. 1 Corinthians 13:12

The Christian writer, Philip Yancey asks why it is that pain is such a big problem when pain's antonym, pleasure, is not a problem at all. Pleasure is what a lot of us live for—without it life would not be tolerable. The obvious answer to Yancey's, very insightful, question is that we don't like pain: physical, psychological or deprivational, and do not think we should have to endure it. Strangely enough we—at least in the West—do not think we should have to endure it because it is not 'right'—as it detracts from a 'better life experience'. And we know when something is 'plainly' wrong. We do not though complain about pleasure; we do not ask why, in fact, we are able to enjoy the sensation of pleasure—in whatever form it takes. Good 'experiences' not an issue though painful experiences may be—depending on how we cope with the—especially people of faith. Oddly enough the Bible does not refer to 'the problem of pain'. Of course, it refers to pain and suffering—with a complete book (Job) on the plight of one man in particular. But, as far as one can see, it does not refer to the 'problem of pain' per se. Pain does not feature in God's list of wrongs. I am not, of course, suggesting that pain was/is thought to be a particular blessing. Pleasure, however, causes all kinds of problems. If we were not able to 'enjoy' things—it follows that we would not desire them—'things' that is. There are desires that drive humans (imago Dei[5]) to commit the most heinous acts; the Biblical Narrative hides none of them. The story of King David, Uriah and his wife Bathsheba is one such story[6].

According to the current understanding of the history of evolutionary physiology , pain is (de facto) a part of the package for particular creatures in the Darwinian concept of 'Tree of Life'—not to be confused with the Tree of Life' in Genesis chapter three. In the Biblical Narrative pain is a dé facto part of living—it, i.e. pain was there at the 'genesis'—though not necessarily at the intensity experienced presently—even in Eden. One can imagine, for example, that there would have been the process of 'seed &

---

[5] Contrary to various views/ideas regarding the meaning of 'imago Dei' (being made in God's image), the view here is that God's image in Humankind is not merely one of 'function' (the sole purpose being one of functionality i.e. 'practical governance') or even of potentiality—i.e. potentiality for a relationship with the Creator. But rather as related to 'certain attributes or characteristics that we share with the Triune God.' (Andrews, 2018).

[6] In summary: King David, a man of authority, a man after God's heart, sees Bathsheba, is rather taken with her, arranges for her husband Uriah to be transferred to the battle front and subsequently killed and then marries her. (2 Samuel chapter 11)

harvest' so there would have been a system in which objects of creation brought forth life and then died (see John 12:24-26)7. Would not an insect, should it have been trodden on and crushed beyond its ability to survive—have ceased to 'live'? Childbirth is an example of the awareness of pain. Genesis 3:16 states that, as a result of the fall, the pain of childbirth would increase; it follows therefore that it [suffering] must have been in existence before The Fall. In Genesis 3:17 'painful toil' is to become the order of the day—they knew what pain because it was, de facto, a part of the 'life experience'. However, as has already suggested and as the text allows for, it does appear that pain did not have the same [agonizing] effects, specifically on highly conscious beings, as it had had prior to the Adamic Fall. It is possible that there might have been a different physiology—that the effects of pain (in all of its expressions) were not as injurious as they were to become.

The very existence of 'sentience' requires pain to be a necessary part of the physiology of life. Pain (the nervous system's reaction to 'intrusions' of various kinds) has always been a part of the 'life-experience' of sentient creatures. I am, mostly, persuaded that pain and suffering existed before the Adamic Fall—but that its effects, as has already been alluded to, **<u>would not have been</u>** so devastating—so all-encompassing—especially in the world outside of 'EDEN'. We most likely disapprove of its existence and, should we have been able, we would most probably have created a world

---

7 John 12:24-26 New International Version (NIV)

without pain. This 'hypothetical' world, however, may not have been a possibility—similar to the imaginary Multiverse[8] that some argue exists. One, therefore could 'go easy' on God and accept that this world may well be the best possible world—a world that is 'fit for God's purpose' and not ours. Evil, we may presume, was the only thing that did not inhabit the paradise of God. Yet, the choice between 'Good & Evil' was ever present in the psyche of the first humans—and indeed in extraterrestrials.

According to the Apostle Paul (Romans 8:20-30) creation was subjected to futility—Paul describes it as 'groaning' and 'longing'. David Bentley Hart translates Romans 8:20 as "…the creation was subordinate to pointlessness…" So we can say that it could be described as anything other than 'the best possible world'—though that would be a judgment given from a blinkered perspective. The best of possible worlds envisaged here is that which God has in mind rather than it being 'our' best of possible environments. With particular regard to humanity, the apostle writes that "…death spread to all men…". (Romans 5:12)The apostle does not refer to other life forms—but specifically to those

---

[8] Multiverse is the term used for an imaginary/hypothetical set of universes which, together, produce reality. 'If not here then—there in another universe'. The idea is supposed to add to the weight of chance over design—that anything can [and does] happen given enough 'time', and that there does not have to be a 'first cause'— God. Of course, should God so desire, he could make available the necessary information for the process to start and finish. Anything is possible with consciousness but with chance—well that's another 'matter' altogether.

of the human race—the imago Dei. Yet creation witnesses something more significant.

The 18th Century, former slave trader, John Newton wrote the hymn entitled 'Amazing Grace'. Newton's life as the captain of a ship transporting African slaves across the Atlantic Ocean, was one of baseness; Newton was a man that cared not for the value of 'a cargo' that was held in such low esteem; the 'humans' being trafficked had no 'value' apart from the gold received for their weight. Then something happened that profoundly changed his life—and ultimately the lives of countless others.

We seem to have been affected or rather infected by the idea that humanity is not perfect but [deep down] 'OK'—that there is nothing wrong with 'Adam's' race (i.e. you and me) that cannot be dealt with—given enough time. However, should the effects of another's moral failure/ineptitude enter into our world we may have a different understanding of the matter as it would then be up close and very personal. It is when it (evil) 'shows up on our doorstep' that we may ask the 'Why Me' question—a question directed at the mysterious notion of 'deity'—in particular the God of Abraham.

That there is a 'flaw' (in the nature of human beings) that not many would argue with—though there would be 'defences' of various genres offered as reasons for such failings. Before Darwin, the cause of this 'imperfection' was, seemingly, easily identified and was traceable to chapter three of the book of Genesis.

The Fall of the original humans was given as the major reason for the existence of both 'Natural' and 'Moral' evil—that as a result of the disobedience of Adam and Eve—thereafter 'all hell broke loose'. Though not excluding the notion of an original pair, that might be considered the progenitors of Modern Humans, the argument here (for the existence of evil) has a different dimension to that of the fall of Adam & Eve per se.

Regarding 'Original Sin':Joel B.Green's view is that although Israel's scriptures are less than replete with theological reflections regarding the ongoing significance of Adam and Eve's disobedience in the Garden, a few Jewish texts from the Second Temple Period[9] do work with Genesis 3 as they tell something of the story of sin. Green notes that these texts agree in two important respects: "(1) Adam (or Eve's) disobedience results in their mortality and in the mortality of all who would come after them, and (2) human beings remain responsible for their actions." (Green, Joel B., 2017)[10]

Stephen Jay Gould, the late paleontologist, held the belief

---

[9] The period between 516BC and 70AD (aka BCE & CE)

[10] Please note that this is, most definitely not, to exclude 'that which is obvious'— that there is a huge 'Moral Dilemma' regarding our species--that many 'noble minds', academics and 'politically minded' individuals continue to, ignore, deny or vehemently argue against—though this is not the place for that particular argument.

that the history of life ... is not going anywhere intrinsically—that we (Homo sapiens) are the accidental result of an unplanned process, in other words, "...the fragile result of an enormous concatenation of improbabilities, not the predictable product of any definite process."i Moreover Gould 'confirmed' that, "...biology has no covering law, or trend, enabling one to say that microbes, or mammals, or men could statistically be expected. Evolutionary theory, he states, offers no explanation of the crucial journey, indeed it claims there is none, but that the results are random. All that is selected for its capacity to survive, unrelated to any increase of worth or value." Of course, this is not just the 'voice' of the late-great paleontologist but the 'natural conclusion' of a materialistic world-view. Contrary to the materialist view of origins etc. the philosopher Alvin Plantinga (2011) rightly points out that, "...it is perfectly possible that the process of [natural] selection has been guided and superintended by God, and that it (natural selection) could not have produced our living world without that guidance." Plantinga refers to the work of the biologist Brian Goodwin, in which Goodwin observes that, It appears that Darwin's theory works for the small-scale aspects of evolution—that it can explain the variations and the adaptations with species that produce fine-tuning of varieties to different habitats—however: "The large-scale differences of form between types of organism that are the foundation of biological classification systems seem to require another principle rather than natural selection operating on small variation, some process that gives rise to distinctly different forms of organism.

This is the problem of emergent order in evolution, the origins of novel structures in organisms, which has always been one of the primary foci of attention in biology.[11]

The storyline throughout this book is one that considers all the difficulties that appear to surround the notion of mankind's relationship with the Creator of the cosmos i.e. created by the God of the Judean Scriptures—and not that of some other 'quirk of the universe' e.g. 'an unidentifiable universal consciousness' (panpsychism) . The argument here is that there is a 'God-Driven Teleology'—a 'goal of creation' that is purposeful rather than chaotic:

> Our willingness to accept scientific claims that are against common sense is the key to an understanding of the real struggle between science and the supernatural. We take the side of science despite the patent absurdity of some of its constructs, in spite of its failure to fulfil many of its extravagant promises of health and life, in spite of the tolerance of the scientific community for unsubstantiated just-so-stories, because we have a prior commitment, a commitment to materialism…It is not that the methods and institutions of science somehow compel us to accept a

---

[11] Goodwin, How the Leopard changed its spots, Princeton: Princeton University Press 1994

material explanation of the phenomenal world but, on the contrary, that we are forced by our a priori adherence to material causes to create an apparatus of investigation and a set of concepts that produce material explanations, no matter how counter-intuitive, no matter how mystifying to the uninitiated. Moreover, that materialism is absolute, for we cannot allow a divine foot in the door. Richard Lewontin[12]

Et ideo non sequitur

---

[12] From a piece in the New York Review of Books (January 9,1997),quoted by J. Budziszewski in 'The Second Tablet Project', First Things (June/July 2002)

INTRODUCTION

The ideas in this book address the Problem of Evil from a biblical perspective as it is the goodness of the God of the Bible that is in question. Consequently, it takes the notion of God's benevolence seriously; it also takes the notion of humankind's image-bearing status seriously. Moreover, it takes the story of the fall of humankind seriously, their banishment from the presence of God and the subsequent consequences for humankind and the rest of creation.

Within the few pages of this book, I shall offer an argument proffering the view that, in spite of the notion of 'Evolution' being an unguided, unrepeatable system 'driven' by an entirely naturally selective process, it has been, mostly, the means through which GOD has brought about a necessary state of affairs. This being a state of affairs that—ultimately leads to the best of possible worlds, in which, in spite of the influence of other minds:

The wolf shall dwell with the lamb, and the leopard shall lie down with the young goat, and the calf and the lion and the fattened calf together; and a little child shall lead them.(Isaiah 11:6)

The Goodness of God, despite the seeming contradictions 'evidenced' by a 'pitiless' production of parasitism, predation, plague and premature death can be defended.

The methodological approach taken in this book is one in which the shape of the account is determined by Christian doctrine—the scientific contribution being critically appropriated to that doctrinally shaped account.
I consider the implications/alternatives espoused by some philosophical theologians—exploring the alternative views of the 'nature' and 'attributes' of God, i.e. the transposition of the God of Scripture with another in the light of the problem of 'natural evil'—that of a creative 'ground of being' rather than the coherent personality offered in Scripture. Further to its research objectives, the argument in this book investigates recent evolutionary defences offered by current proponents, and others, of both scientific enquiry and theological research and reflection.

A significant part of the argument in this book centres on the strong possibility of the pre-cosmological existence of angels—as well as the rebellion of those angels, considered 'fallen'.

The argument offered here is that such creatures have been at the root of the universal problem of evil (natural and supernatural) since before the 'birthing' of the universe. It is further argued that the problem of evil was dealt a fatal blow through the incarnational work of God, i.e. The sacrificial work of Christ on the Cross and Christ's resurrection from the dead.

> And he who was seated on the throne said, 'Behold, I am making all things new.' Also, he said, 'Write this down, for these words are trustworthy and true.' (Revelation 21:5)

It isn't so much an interest in seeking a resolution to 'the problem of evil' (Natural Evil and Moral Evil) but rather a concern to offer an account of the reason why evil exists and, most importantly, why the God of the Judean/Christian Scriptures allows it to both exist and to continue—seemingly 'ad infinitum'. The God in question isn't some 'lower-order' demiurge 'creator' (as in Platonic Philosophy) . On the contrary, I am referencing the creator and sustainer of all things, i.e. The God who is Omniscient, Omnipotent and Benevolent; and this in the light of an evolutionary process that is, seemingly, the root cause of suffering--a process referred to as 'natural'—a process that may be described as that through which "…thousands of animals are being eaten alive; others are running for their lives, whimpering with fear; others are being slowly devoured from within by rasping parasites…" [etc.] (Dawkins, 1996)

The word benevolence is, as McCabe (2010) reports Aquinas as saying, "…used *'secundum analogiam'* (according to analogy)…The inferences in the case of God fail because 'good' is a contextually dependent word."—Moreover, the creative processes that brought about the biosphere is a case in point, i.e. making uninformed judgements regarding God's benevolence. Though it is the case that Aquinas thought that evil was, most often, the absence (privation) of positive outcomes. It can be argued that to say that God's benevolence always has to be interpreted as God's having to bring about 'good' outcomes for whosoever—whether justified outcomes or not is mistaken; this does not abrogate God's right to forgive (or not) but God's right to bring about a just state of affairs.

Evolution here is taken to be the process through which [God], rather than entirely unguided 'law driven' material processes, has brought about the 'necessary' conditions for the development of life and consciousness. Dennis Lamoureux (2013) offers an evolutionary theological perspective that he refers to as 'Evolutionary Creation', "Evolutionary creation asserts that the Father, Son, and Holy Spirit created the universe and life, including humans, through an ordained, sustained and intelligent design-reflecting evolutionary process." It is from the perspective of a 'purposeful' process that my argument is developed— although my opinions differ somewhat from those of an

'Evolutionary Creationist'.

Since the advent of Darwinism—and because of the increasing challenge of Naturalistic Materialism—there is an increasingly urgent need for a fresh approach to the subject of theodicy, i.e. 'the vindication of divine providence given the presence of evil'. As a result of a developing (hostile) narrative, the existence of the God of the Bible is in question or simply classified along with 'fairy story' narratives—as being blatantly false.

The second reason for the undertaking of the research, and the publication of this book is because of a personal dissatisfaction with 'Fall Defences' aka 'narratives'—defences that offer the actions of the 'original humans' as the, God ordained, catalyst for the predation, parasitism and plague experienced by all carbon-based life-forms (according to some) not more than 10,000 years ago, i.e. since the disobedience of the first humans. NB.I am equally dissatisfied with defences that offer naturalistic explanations, philosophical speculation or dialectical reasoning—without major consideration for that which Scripture may teach regarding past and future events. This book is concerned with framing an overall picture of what shall be termed as the '*Telos of God*'(God's GOAL). In the process of developing the argument I consider the extent to which suffering acts as a charge against either the power or the goodness of God.

This book addresses the problem from a position of belief and commitment to a view of God's character and attributes—as offered by the Scriptures rather from any monistic or modern/post-modern notion of the 'person'/character of God. The argument here offers what may be considered a fresh approach to the problem—an approach which is consistent both with the Scriptures and with a–creative-evolutionary view of God's 'eternal' perspectives, i.e. His 'plans and purposes' for the created order.

The approach to this work is of a 'theological-philosophical' nature rather than a purely philosophical approach. The reasons for taking this approach are due, in particular, to the nature of the 'charge' against God—not any 'god' but, specifically, the God of the Bible, i.e. that 'biological-evolutionary-processes' cannot be harmonised with any notion of divine benevolence.

Methodological Considerations

The approach to the subject matter of this book is situated in relation to the taxonomy offered by Neil Messer (2007). Messer considers five possible options:

Option 1: Only science contributes to the account, and the contribution of Christian doctrine is dismissed. This option has no bearing on this work as it is, primarily, a theological work that discusses a scientific given—that of Evolutionary Theory.

Option 2: Both science and Christian doctrine contribute to the account; its shape is determined by the scientific contribution, and the input from Christian doctrine must be adjusted to fit the outlines determined by the scientific contribution.

NB. This approach cannot be the one taken here. It is Christian doctrine that is the determining factor—for it is with Christian doctrine that the challenge presently lies.

Option 3: Both science and Christian doctrine contribute, and neither has sole control over the shape of the account. *This option is partly acceptable. However, as conservative Christian beliefs are based on Scripture and tradition—that which has been affirmed by the conciliar creeds, as a reliable and, indeed, plausible account of the history of God's interaction with humankind—Scripture rather than scientific interpretation should have the final word. This is not to suggest that the evolutionary paradigm may be deficient (though it may be proven to be so), but rather that it is a matter of doctrine over science; this is of particular importance as it is likely that, as scientific paradigms develop, the more 'accurate or more reliable model' will be accepted as being superior to the prevailing paradigm. Ideas change and paradigms may change along with those ideas. Faith, on the other hand, does not depend on scientific verification but adherence to the doctrine revealed in the Scriptures and attested by the great councils of the Church.*

Option 4: Both science and Christian doctrine contribute; the shape of the account is determined by Christian doctrine, and the scientific contribution is critically appropriated to that doctrinally shaped account. *This is crucial for this thesis—this particular type of encounter'—in which both science and Christian doctrine contribute to the account, its shape being determined by Christian doctrine, and the scientific contribution being critically appropriated to that doctrinally shaped account...'*

Option 5: Only the contribution of Christian doctrine is admitted, the scientific contribution being denied or dismissed. *This option is not relevant to this research project, since, in broad terms, the scientific relevance of an evolutionary narrative is not presently in question.*

The 'Christian persuasion' is summed up by the following:

That Scripture (The Bible) is the final authority in all matters of faith and doctrine (Sola Scriptura). That is not to deduce that the Scriptures are the product of 'divine dictation'—to quote Alister McGrath: "Just as Christ's divinity does not abrogate Christ's human nature, so the divine authorship of Scripture does not abolish its human authorship." (McGrath, 1993)

It is appreciated that 'no one proposition' may express all the truth, but the notion that there is, therefore, no likelihood of any such truths is not denied. The author advocates belief in the propositional nature of Scripture, e.g. 'Jesus Christ is Lord';

'Humans are Sinful'; 'Jesus' death atones for human sin'; 'There is Judgement'. (Groothius, 2000). "…The Christian gospel tells how for the world's redemption God entered into history,…'the eternal came into time, the kingdom of heaven invaded the realm of earth, in the significant events of the incarnation, crucifixion, and resurrection of Jesus the Christ." (Bruce, 1960) The truth of Christian doctrine does not depend solely on personal belief or the beliefs of the community of faith; it is true whether or not anyone adheres to its propositions.

The importance of personal encounter/experience of God is a given, though it is not advocated that experience is the sole witness of the work of God, or that it should have pre-eminence as the principal means of the witness of the individual believer or the community of faith.

Fundamental to my approach to the subject of evolutionary theodicy is the belief that the Testaments of the Bible are trustworthy in all things essential for faith. Gordon Wenham (1987) says, regarding any perceived problem of the received wisdom of the distant past and of the (post) modern present:

> If it is correct to view Genesis 1-11 as an inspired retelling of ancient oriental traditions about the origins of the world—with a view to presenting the nature of the true God as one, omnipotent, omniscient, and good as opposed to the fallible, capricious, weak deities who populated the rest of

the ancient world; if furthermore it is concerned to show that humanity is central in the divine plan, not afterthought; if finally, it wants to show that man's plight is the product of his [own] disobedience and indeed is bound to worsen without divine intervention, Genesis 1-11 is setting a picture of the world that is at odds both with the polytheistic optimism of ancient Mesopotamia and with the humanistic secularization of the (post) modern world.

In the introduction to his book 'The Lost World of Genesis One' (2009) John Walton says of the Old Testament, that "…it is God's revelation of himself to Israel and secondarily through Israel to everyone else." Walton affirms the distinctiveness of the biblical literature when compared to other contemporary writings. Indeed Walton suggests that to compare the Old Testament to the literature of the ancient world is not, "…to assume that we expect to find similarity at every point." The Bible is, as Walton states, distinctive—in that it does reveal the nature and character of God. Moreover, Scripture is, as the apostle Paul makes clear in his letter to Timothy:"…breathed out by God and profitable for teaching…"(2 Timothy 3:16).It is the case that though the Bible uses various literary devices (metaphors, similes etcetera), this does not imply that it conveys indecisive language or that it does not include historical narrative. It is also the case that although the Bible is not a textbook of science, it informs us of the relation of God to the cosmos and human beings.

It is not that the Bible is offering some kind of 'scientific treatise' from which we can deduce equations. It means that Scripture reveals certain truths but not others. Examples of such truths would be the essential [high] calling of humankind in God's creative purposes, and the redeeming work of Christ—and of God's immanent, cruciform relationship with his creation throughout the history of the cosmos. In addition to the above, the following commitments are an essential part of the argument given here in this book:

o That God is sovereign over the universe and all that functions within it: that this sovereign God is not to be confused with lesser gods—demiurges. Moreover, that the sovereign God has allowed evil to exist on earth so that evil is ultimately defeated. the emergence of creatures with the 'will to choose, within the created order, was a major part of God's goal for the creation. **NB**. The notion/possibility of the absence of Free-Will in advanced, sentient beings such as humankind, would be in contradistinction to the character of the God who is the ultimate expression of personality and unity.

o That the Goodness of God is coterminous with the justice of God, and the Justice of God entails God's desire to 'deliver from evil' rather than to exert a 'compensatory' form of justice—though God's ultimate justice must prevail in whatever form God so chooses.

- o That the laws of physics (as presently understood) are fundamental to God's creation of the cosmos,and of the ensuing evolution of biological life forms.
- o That, despite what might be considered a flawed physical system (i.e. a flaw in the laws of physics) it is the preordained purposes of God that an evolutionary process should be the means through which God would bring about his eternal purposes [ultimately] at the eschaton.

NB. *It is, most definitely not to say, that what is, presently, known or observed of the evolutionary process is in any way the 'whole story'.*

Arguing for the Goodness of God in the light of the ongoing saga of life is an undeniably high hurdle to overcome yet it is not an insurmountable obstacle.

THIS IS THE TASK UNDERTAKEN IN THIS BOOK.

Soli Deo Gloria

PART 1

GOOD

Four Letter Words

It is most likely a coincidence that some of the most profane and profound words in the English language only have four letters; more than likely several words come to mind—words that, nowadays, form a part of General English Usage. Here are four others that may not have immediately come to mind: 'evil', 'good', 'love' and 'pain'. All four of these words have a connection. Love can cause both pain and evil. Pain is often thought to be the result of evil—something: inflicted, by God, as punishment for wrongdoing, by another party as an act of malevolence or as the consequence of a physiological malfunction. Evil could be considered a kind of generic term for many of the world's ills.

The Oxford English Dictionary defines the word 'Evil' both as an adjective and as a noun: Adjective: (a) deeply immoral and malevolent. (b) embodying or associated with the devil. (c) Extremely unpleasant Noun. (a) Extreme wickedness and depravity, especially when regarded as a supernatural force. (b) Something harmful or undesirable. As a matter of interest, Evil spelt backwards, is 'live', sideways it is 'veil'—inside-out it is 'vile'. (2005)

For those who affirm the notion that God is GOOD, the evidence, from the (human) perspective, for that goodness remains rather elusive. The Problem of Evil is most certainly a barrier to faith, i.e. the problem of how it is possible for God to have allowed for the evolution of life on earth and to retain his goodness— remains a mystery. However, 'the problem of evil' is not usually perceived as a personal problem—something related to me personally—that 'I' might, in some way, be culpable. doctoral dissertations and bookshelves are replete with titles such as 'Evil and the Goodness of God', 'Goodness, Omnipotence and Suffering', or 'God is not Great'. God, it seems, has had too much bad press at the hands (computers) and from the mouths of those who think that God is unjust or simply cannot exist as the contradictions are far too great. Regarding human behaviour though, we often say that this or that action is not acceptable, that it is morally reprehensible. We make all kind of moral pronouncements.

There does seem to be a kind of 'universal', give or take the odd differences, sense of 'right and wrong'—almost as if God, at some time in our evolutionary development, had instilled (as it were) into our actual DNA the knowledge of the difference between good and not good—evil even. We know instinctively when human behaviour has exceeded the boundaries of acceptability though we are keen to move the boundaries as we become increasingly disconnected from our creator. Moreover, we so often ignore the symptoms that are a sign that death rather than life is at work in us. Evil for so many of us, professing Christians included, is something unrelated to us; we see it as an abstract thing that has no connection with us or with the rest of the human race. Of course, 'evil' itself has no substance—though, as I have previously argued, evil has a 'personification' as it manifests itself—and is, mostly, identifiable as the result of moral failure on behalf of members or a member of the human race. Though, as I have argued, it is not only corporeal creatures that we can, justifiably, apportion blame—as we so often wish to blame GOD.

Evil and the Goodness of God is such a 'vast' subject, a subject that fills the shelves of libraries; indeed many have devoted their lives to attempting to resolve it. The question of, how an alleged God of Love, who is 'All Powerful', can allow such evil to continue to exist is one that will not go away. But why is it that we humans have the temerity to demand an explanation from God or to doubt the existence of the God of the Bible because we find [this particular] God under qualified or wanting? Doesn't it strike one as rather odd that our very argument against God's goodness comes from the notion of the actual existence of 'good and evil'—a belief that owes its origins to the Judeo/Christian Scriptures—and a malevolence that has its origins in another source. What guarantee have we that these precious social mores (that we in the 'West' take for granted) do not evaporate 'overnight' under the weight of 'other ideas'—ideas that are socially engineered and not universally absolute? Of course many societies adhere to other ideas—ideas that see 'black as white and white as black'—yet there is a strange notion of injustice at the 'heart'—and that is because of the existence of GOD—The Alpha and Omega: 'who was and is and is to come.' (Revelation 1:8)

No other 'GOOD'

In this section I shall, briefly, address, what may be considered the 'straw men' (demeaning caricatures) of modern and post-modern attempts at lessening the culpability of the classical 'image' of God in the light of evolutionary theory—and also in the light of contemporary religious and philosophical notions of the reality of God. The views offered here are considered incontrovertibly necessary to the defence of the God of the Bible against other notions and ideas that may be seen a better fit the evolutionary paradigm but that only serve to remove the problem by the substitution of the God of Scripture with a lesser 'deity'.

The God portrayed and 'defended' in this book is the God of the Judeo/Christian Scriptures. A God whose eternity, Peter Sanlon (2014) describes as a qualitatively different kind of existence to one of his creatures: "Being outside of time does not mean that God cannot know what happens inside of time, nor that he cannot interact with a temporal order. Quite the opposite! It does, of course, shape the way he does these things." As Sanlon makes clear in the same passage "It would perhaps be odd for him to create something with which he could not interact. Similarly, God created time. It is part of the created order. And though God is not himself temporal, he can interact with and know all that occurs in, the times he has made. Indeed, precisely because God is not temporal, he has perfect knowledge of all events in time." This God is not to be confused with any other ideas/notions/ theologies or philosophies of God —either pre-modern, modern or post-modern—as shall be made clear throughout the development of this argument.

In developing his argument regarding 'The Mind of God', (2013) Hart refers to "…provocatively counterintuitive ways of expressing the difference between God and every contingent reality—that God, as the source of all being, is, properly speaking, not himself a being—or, if one prefer, not a being among other beings…that God is no particular thing, or even 'no thing'…or even, as *ein lauter Nichts*'—a 'pure nothingness." The above, as Hart points out, though 'appearing blasphemous or paradoxical', is meant to give us pause for thought and reflection on the 'nature' and person of GOD—"…in order to remind us as forcibly as possible that God is not to be found within the realm of things, for he is the being of all realms." (Bentley Hart, 2013)

Constraints on God

Should God be limited in his ability to produce or concoct the best possible plans for fulfilling his creative objectives, God would not be omnipotent. Christopher Southgate argues that the sort of universe we have, in which complexity emerges in a process governed by thermodynamic necessity and Darwinian natural selection is the only sort of universe that could give rise to all that the earth has produced. To affirm an evolutionary process as being 'the only way' through which God could achieve his objectives one has to assume that God was unable (lacked the ability) to bring about his creative objectives, i.e. without this astronomical/ biological framework ,or that God's use of such a process was the best possible means through which God could bring about the best of possible outcomes. The aforementioned is, a similar point to the one noted in Alexander, (2008) that sees biology as a 'package deal': If biology should be a 'stand-alone-package-deal,' i.e. a package deal that has no significance other than it being the product of creative genius; then it is reasonable to suppose that the creator's benevolent characteristics could be called into question— unless there is more to the story other than God's desire to create.

I am, of course, assuming that there has been an intentional pathway within the evolutionary process otherwise there would be no reason to suppose that any such future outcomes could be considered anything other than random outcomes within the naturally selective process of evolution.

Jeff Astley (2009) asks whether or not God could have ordered nature differently and then answers his question by saying, 'perhaps not'. Astley goes on to say however that materiality inevitably involves imperfection—a tendency to disorder, decay, fragility, and mortality. Astley's point is significant as it is the case that the accusation against the 'designer God' is often that of incompetence—the design is simply under par or faulty. Ergo, God is either impotent or fails to meet the necessary criteria or the presuppositions of the complainant. This assertion is false as shall be argued in another part of this book. Keith Ward's (1990) comments are insightfully apposite when he refers to 'natural' evil as 'an inevitable consequence of this kind of world'. I hasten to add here though—that it is not that this world is governed solely by 'natural forces' but that this world is probably the only possible world in which carbon-based-life could obtain and the telos of the Triune God be established. Moreover, there are other [unseen] forces that bring about deleterious effects on the biosphere (even the physical laws) through means that are, presently, beyond the comprehension of any material analysis.

Questions of Ontological Veracity

In this section I shall briefly, though importantly, address the notion of 'God' as the ground of being rather than as a determinate entity; in other words that the creation, though not purely the product of chance and necessity, was not the 'design product' of personality/personal ingenuity.

Should the term 'God' refer only to a 'ground of being' first cause, i.e. a first cause that defies description or a 'first cause' that may be loosely described as 'nature'—then there would be no case to answer for the existence of evil—at least not on 'god's' part, because there would be no personal creative-agent against whom a charge may be brought. It is the case that,should the term 'God' refer only to a 'ground of being' first cause—a first cause that defies description or that may be loosely described as 'One' as in Pantheistic Monism or as 'Nature' as in Naturalism and Atheistic Materialism then there is no case to answer—for there is, indeed, no personal agent that may be found guilty of failure of any sort. The notion of a 'Ground of Being', presumably, thought by its advocates, to deal with, what might be considered, as more intellectually coherent case for 'god' or that might better fit with the problem of natural evil , does nothing of the sort apart from demeaning the God of the Bible. However, it is such a view that is commonly espoused by philosophical theologians such as Wesley Wildman. Wildman opines (2011) that any notion of 'ultimate reality' is bizarre but adds that 'most theologians and a few philosophers are captivated by such (ultimate reality) speech' and that they even choose it while understanding its 'final futility'. In his section on 'Determinate-Entity Theism' Wildman, regarding this alleged futility, asks what kind of entity the divine reality is? The conclusion is that the God of the Bible seems to be made in the image of its authors (not an original thought). In short, God's determinate nature is known in our longings. Everything else we say theologically (Wildman suggests) must serve this overridingly important version of ultimate reality, and this (according to Wildman et al.) becomes the crucial criterion of determinate-entity theism. Wildman's ideas seem to have little to do with any perceived notion of the goodness of the Triune God of Scripture as Wildman's picture of God bears no resemblance whatsoever to this God. Wildman's rationale seems to be that, "Speaking of God as The Ground of Being removes the possibility of proposing a divine character that is profoundly different from the character of the world." i.e. the evolved/evolving biosphere.

Wildman is correct in his assertion that "Determinate-entity theism requires a divine goodness that our best scientific vision of the cosmos does not easily support, and so positively requires some ontological distance between God and the world and a layer of theological explanation for why the world is the way it appears to be—despite the purported impeccability of God's moral character." I agree with Wildman when he says that, "Ground-of-being theism needs neither to explain a discrepancy nor to distinguish among events to articulate the divine nature." (Wildman 2007). The question needs to be voiced: Is this a valid reason for the 'fabrication' of a 'god' made in the image of other theologies or of 'prevailing ' world-views?

Wildman's views are clearly expressed. Indeed, it would seem that the notion of God as a 'determinate entity' creates huge philosophical questions—especially with regards to the problem of [natural] evil. It is, of course, possible that the God revealed in the Bible is a figment of the imaginative wishful thinking of latter-day 'hominins'—particularly the authors of the Old Testament. Wildman states that the 'divine goodness' described in the Scriptures is a 'difficult fit' with the apparent evidence.

However, it is striking that many distinguished theologians and philosophers are content to hold to a more classical approach.

Keith Ward (2008) comments that to call God good is to say that God actualizes within himself the best of all possible perfections—moreover, Ward suggests that "If such a God produces a universe like this, then God remains good, whatever the universe may be considered. A supremely good God might, then, necessarily create this universe, or some universe with similar characteristics." By 'necessarily', I take it that Ward means that the sovereign God chose to create this universe in order to bring about the best of possible circumstances, i.e. the 'best possible world'.

However, this does not imply lesser capabilities on God's part, but rather that this world is the best of possible worlds in which God's ultimate 'Good' purposes can be achieved.

As far as Biblical Theism is concerned, there should be no willingness to dilute God's attributes; however, should there be any attempts at 'dilution' the most likely candidates would be those of omniscience, omnipotence or benevolence. Should God be declared 'less knowing' or 'not quite as powerful' as previously thought, the question of God's benevolence becomes less crucial. Any deity that is neither omniscient or omnipotent cannot be held responsible for that which is outside the scope of its influence. The attributes of omniscience and omnipotence, however, remain crucial to any theodicy that takes the legitimacy of the biblical narratives seriously. The 'God is not omniscient or omnipotent' view, in removing the notion of omniscience and omnipotence from the 'stage',leaves room only for the God of Open Theism or even worst: the 'god' of Process Theology/Monism.

For proponents of this position, the argument is likely to be that God does not have the necessary characteristics that enable God to behave with consistent benevolence—leaving room only for dualism or impersonal monism.

Wildman gives an outline of the possibilities: Firstly, he makes clear in his view that, (a) a personal, benevolent, attentive, and active deity cannot create through evolution and (b) that therefore God the creator is not a personal, benevolent, attentive, and active deity. He states that we can preserve those affirmations symbolically (for whatever reason), but goes on to say that:

> … they no longer refer to a divine being with intentions and awareness, with feelings and intelligence, with plans and powers to act; rather, they refer to the ground of being itself, to the creative and fecund power source in the depths of nature, to the value structures and potentialities that the world manifests. They refer to the God beyond God, which is to say the truly ultimate reality that hovers behind and beneath and beyond the symbolic gods we create and deploy to satisfy our personal needs, to make sense of our world, and to legitimate the exercise of social control. (2011)

There is neither time or space to discuss Wildman's assertion that the God of the Bible could not have created through an evolutionary process, though I disagree entirely with Wildman's conclusions. However, it is accepted that this does offer, to some extent, a challenge regarding providence within the evolutionary process. Wildman's 'god' though lacks 'substance' lacks any notion of benevolence—indeed lacks anything in real terms. *Naturally*, this 'god' cannot manifest personal concern for the products of any likely creative processes because this 'ground of being factory' has no 'mind' and no personality from which to proceed. Nevertheless, Wildman's alternative is somehow able to 'allow for' the transformation of the material in the cosmos that, in turn, allowed for the evolution of the biosphere.

Wildman's apparent disillusionment with the biblical notion of God seems to have provoked him to strong language. Clayton and Knapp (2007) make the following reference to Wildman's disdain, quoting him thus: "Frankly, and I say this with the utmost reverence, the personal God does not pass the test of parental moral responsibility. If God is personal in this way, then we must conclude that God has a morally abysmal record of inaction or action."[13]

Wildman's view, as pictured here, offers a not dissimilar view to Sigmund Freud. Freud's view offered by Nicholi (Nicholi, 2002)—that the very idea of 'an idealised Superman' in the sky— is so patently infantile and so foreign to reality seems, most likely, to stem from a total miscomprehension—even caricature of the God of the Bible. It is no doubt the case that some may naively interpret the biblical notion of God in the way that Freud expresses;but some (an increasing number even) may, due to this kind of reasoning or lack of a plausible notion of the God of the Bible, wish to find an alternative 'god'; this, is totally the wrong

---

[13] Wildman says, regarding the use of the word 'evil', that 'suffering is a more useful category than evil because suffering is more neutrally descriptive and does not prejudge the moral character of...[?] regarding natural disasters, predation and the like'. Here, Wildman may well be correct.

direction to take as it leads to another path—a path void of any notion of 'God' whatsoever—at least to anything other than an unworthy caricature of the God that Scripture reveals.

Wildman's view is that 'ground-of-being theologies' are important because of their denial that ultimate reality can 'possibly' be a determinate entity—that this establishes a valuable theological contrast with determinate entity theisms. The 'ground-of-being' view of the 'personhood' of God as well as God's possible interaction with the world may, as Wildman suggests, produce an enthusiastic intellectual response to these pervasive evils. But, at the same time, this view favors, what Wildman considers to be, philosophical logic over and above the revelation of Scripture.

Wildman, I suggest, is mistaken in his deliberations—his alternative 'deity' an unreasonable caricacture. It is unacceptable for two reasons. Firstly, as a result of his dissatisfaction/ disappointment with the 'performance' of the God of the Bible Wildman offers an extra-biblical, pantheistic alternative. Secondly, the substituted, 'ground of being', alternative, fails to convince us that 'it' has any substance whatsoever.

Regarding, the 'narrative to Scripture', Peter Sanlon, rightfully says that:

> [F]or the drama to be of any significance whatsoever there must be real actors in the play. If the metaphor of a drama

has to be developed further, then it must be insisted that the scriptwriter is also real. The God who creates, speaks, directs, interacts and participates must be a real person before he can do any of these things. In technical terminology, ontology is prior to revelation and salvation. Systematic theology recognizes this, and asks the entirely appropriate questions 'What kind of being is he?' And: What may we know of him from his words and actions? (2014)

God is the Triune 'determinate entity' who has created all things and who sustains all things for His 'good' purposes. Ergo, the God of Scripture is the ultimate ontological reality.

Process Thought and Omnipotence

In this section we take a cursory glance at process theology as it applies to 'omnipotence'.

Cobb & Griffin (1976) state the dominant position of process theologians clearly enough when they pose the question of why evil exists when there is in existence, according to classical and biblical theology, a God with 'controlling power'—suggesting that:

> … a major reason that Christian theism has clung on so long to the notions of God as a Controlling Power is that thereby it can assure believers that God's will, despite

appearances, is victorious—for the sake of this assurance it has risked seeing God as the author of needless suffering and even moral evil. It has risked the implicit denial of human freedom and the rebellion of humanistic atheism. (1976)

There is something to be said for this critique. However, the above depiction is an extreme caricature and it is not the picture of sovereignty that is anywhere near to that adhered to by the author of this book—or even of 'Open Theism', which offers freedom without, mostly, denying the overall sovereignty of God[14]. Indeed, the Process interpretation of God offers a rather simplistic view of sovereign reality as it does not allow any means with which to comprehend any notion of ontological veracity for this alleged 'ground of being' other than that of a nebulous force akin to that of pantheism. Indeed, it does not offer anywhere near sufficient reason to replace the God of Scripture with any 'straw man' scenario in the form of dialectical hypothesis. Wildman acknowledges the difficulty in that whatever God is, on the process account, it is exceedingly resistant to anthropomorphic modelling,

---

[14] According to Clark Pinnock, "God as the creator of the world (italics mine) can make the kind of world he likes—in this case a world with free creatures in it…God exercises power in ways appropriate to the creation project…He gives creatures the room decides things and binds himself to the promises he makes. Thus God exercises sovereignty by sharing power not by dominion…God uses omnipotence to 'free' and not enslave…It takes omnipotence to create and manage freedom..." (Pinnock 2000)

'and certainly nothing like the personal God of so many sacred texts and religious pieties'. Wildman 's summary accurately describes the problem from both perspectives.

The God of process theology is considered to be a God that does not abuse, or 'coerce' but persuades—throughout nature and in living beings. The God of process theology cannot override free will; it is not that he (it) will not but rather that he (it) 'Can Not' (can not as in does not have the potency to so do). According to Griffin & Lubarsky (1996) the redefining of the omnipotence of God may be the solution that dissolves the problem of evil as there is no likelihood of culpability on the part of this particular notion of God. Any possibility of continued adherence to the biblical view of omnipotence is ruled out as is made clear from the following, rather long but pertinent, quotation from Griffin:

> Because our universe was created out of chaos rather than out of absolute nothingness, so that creative power is inherent in the world (as well as in God), the creatures' twofold creative power of self-determination and efficient causation cannot be cancelled, overridden, or completely controlled by God. On this basis, process philosophy denies the second premise in the argument…saying instead that although God is all-powerful—not only in the sense of being the supreme power of the universe but also in the sense of being perfect in power, having all the power one being could possibly have—God cannot unilaterally

prevent all evil. If being 'all-powerful' is taken to mean being omnipotent in the sense of essentially having all the power, however, then process philosophy simply denies the first premise's assertion that a being worthy of the name God is all-powerful by definition. (2001)

Both the logic and implication of this kind of thinking is clear. There is, according to this view, in the world of matter (matter that pre-existed the emergence of 'god') an inherent creative capability out of which appears the process of evolution—a process that 'God' could not interfere with but only persuade. So it is from within the alleged 'inherent creative capability' of matter itself that the force of evolution manifests itself (ex nihilo, nihil fit)—and not out of the MIND of the God of Scripture—ex nihilo. Griffin states that 'God', though having all the power possible, does not possess 'ALL POWER' and therefore is not capable of preventing evil or of much else regarding the biological evolutionary process.[15] In contradistinction to the views espoused by Griffin, Wildman et el,.

John Leslie (1989) suggests that: "Neoplatonism is [today] often expressed in such a formula as that God is not a being but the Power of Being. On my interpretation, what dark sayings say that

-----

[15] Madden & Hare (1987) conclude that God is, "...unable to move toward an aesthetic end and without an enormous cost in pain (his own and others); he is apparently so weak that he cannot guarantee his own welfare. If he is that weak, obviously he is not able as a theistic God should be, to ensure the ultimate triumph of an end of his choice."(29)

God is the world's ethical requiredness or, equivalently, that God is the creatively effective ethical need that there should exist a (good) world." (Leslie, 1989) The idea that any such imagined requiredness could exist as a de facto state of affairs—'conjured up' as a more convenient replacement for the God of Biblical Theology—is hardly convincing. Moreover, the notion that ethical principles (or any other come to that) are likely to emanate from anything other than the actual character [Mind] of The God, who is by His very nature 'the ultimate good' is equally unconvincing. Here, we are in agreement with Gregory Boyd (2001) who suggests that "…unless God's essential nature is necessary and actual—apart from his interaction with the world, neither the enduring nature of God nor the contingent nature of the world can be rendered intelligible. God must be self-sufficient within himself, creating and relating to the world out of love instead of metaphysical necessity."

In the light of the problem of creaturely suffering the process 'alternative' may seem an attractive proposition—one that may fit in with some current understandings of reality—but it cannot be taken as the final word regarding the God of the Bible as it fails miserably to do justice to the character of that God. This view of God, 'helpfully', dissolves the problem of evil. A God with restricted or limited ability can hardly be held responsible for failing to address the problem of suffering in any significant way. Indeed, this 'god', it could be said, cannot entertain any kind of

'planned intention'—vis a vis the creation of anything much—
most certainly not creation ex nihilo. This 'god' though could not
be mistaken for the God of the Judeo/Christian Scriptures as this
view of God is a step into the unknown and 'unknowable', and is
not a God we could visualize and, most certainly is nothing like the
Triune God of the Bible.

Paul Copan and William Lane Craig offer a helpful
summary regarding the difference between 'abstract' and
'concrete' objects:

> We have seen that God, though immaterial and
> spatiotemporal, would be classed by everyone as a concrete
> object in view of his being a personal causal agent. Perhaps
> that provides a clue to the distinction between concrete and
> abstract entities. It is virtually universally agreed that
> abstract objects, if they exist, are causally impotent; they do
> not stand in causal relations. Numbers, for example, do not
> effect anything. (Copan, 2004)

Goodness in the Hebrew Scriptures

In this section, the use of the word 'good' in Scripture is
considered in reasonable detail, in particular with regards to its use
in the Genesis narrative—how this word is ascribed to the God of
the Bible and to the creation. Ben Mitchel notes that "Grounded in
the biblical text and the theology of the Fathers of the Church, it is

not too strong to say—that 'when God made the world it was good'—has been the dominant view among orthodox Christians (although there have been divergent views on the length of the time designated by a day)." (2018)

In looking at the Genesis creation narrative (Genesis 1:1-2:3) C. J. Collins (2006) notes that the author of Genesis refers to God looking back at what he had created—stated that "behold, it was very good" (1:31). Collins, referring to Thomas Aquinas, writes that, he [God] brought things into being—and that his goodness might be communicated to his creatures, and be represented by them. Yamauchi (2003) outlines five areas of 'good' (tōv): practical, abstract, quality, moral, and technical. Melvin Tinker (2010) refers to the use of the word 'good' (tōv) and the conditioning of the word in context—suggesting that:

> …while the word has many shades of meaning, ranging from 'useful to 'beautiful' to 'valuable', the meaning of the word in any particular case will be conditioned, to a large extent, by its immediate context. It can certainly mean 'aesthetically good' and need not mean 'perfection'…in the context of Genesis 1 the meaning is best taken as 'efficient'…This interpretation leaves room for the idea of a creation which is perfectly in line with what the creator intended but which is less than absolutely perfect,… (2010)

Ronald E. Osborn (2014) suggests that, as unsettling as it may be for some readers to discover that nowhere in Genesis is the creation described as 'perfect', "God declares his work to be good or *tob* at each stage and finally very good i.e. *tob me 'od* at its end. Elsewhere in The Hebrew Bible tob me 'od describes qualities of beauty, worthiness or fitness for a purpose but never absolute moral or ontological perfection." In his comments on Genesis 1:31 Umberto Cassuto states that:

> …we have here, at the conclusion of the story of creation, a more elaborate and imposing statement that points to the general harmony prevailing in the world of the Almighty. On the previous days the words that it was good were applied to a specific detail; now God saw everything that He had made, the creation in its totality, and He perceived that not only were the details, taken separately, good, very good, but that each one harmonized with the rest; hence the whole was not just good, but very good. (1998)

It would seem, prima facie, most incongruous, if the state of affairs Cassuto describes, could be that of the 'genesis' of the evolutionary process but that would be to miss the point—for the Genesis narrative (1:31) states that, on the sixth day, "God saw everything he had made, and behold, it was very good." The question is: Would it have been a time for rejoicing for an Omnipotent & Omniscient creator with any semblance of morality in his character?

Moreover, It is clear from (and according to) the Genesis text that God concluded, on 'the sixth day', that the creation was, indeed, 'very good'. The question arises as to how this 'very goodness' can apply to an evolutionary creation. The key is in the literary function of the, "And God said" phrases—sometimes referred to as 'divine fiats'—occurring, as they do, at least nine times in chapter one of Genesis.

Physicist Alan Hayward (1985) suggests that though the [Genesis] text doesn't tell us, there is a suggestion in the [Job] narrative that the audience of God's creative declarations may have been angels (Job 38:4-7). Hayward's point is that God does not see things the way man sees them and that, to God, "...the fiats are real; once the word is spoken, the deed is certain to follow. He commanded, and at once he saw—in his mind's eye, so to speak...from the perspective of Heaven it seems that foreordaining something is tantamount to creating it." It is in this sense that God can conclude—and that the author of Genesis can record—that the creation was, is and will be, 'Very Good'. Making reference to the laws of physics, in particular the Second Law of Thermodynamics, Hayward comments that the Second Law does not denote a universe where things have gone wrong but that, "It characterizes a universe where energy transfers can occur, and consequently where things can happen—in other words, a 'very good' universe." A world where the Second law did not operate would be, in Hayward's opinion, stagnant.

Christopher Southgate (2008) refers to the beautiful rhythms of the first chapter of the Hebrew Bible that culminate in the assertion that what God had made was 'very good'. Southgate, however, points out that we humans have always known that the creation contained 'violence and pain' and accepts that there is a real problem in affirming with Genesis 1:31 that this creation is "very good". He nevertheless holds that creation is good: "—in its propensity to give rise to great values of beauty, diversity, complexity, and ingenuity of evolutionary strategy." Southgate makes clear nevertheless that these kinds of values do not of themselves act as justification for creation by means of the 'recognized' evolutionary process. It is agreed that creation's propensity to give rise to 'great values' is a 'good'. The view in this book though is that God's 'very good' refers not to the beginnings of the creation [process], but the whole of God's planned intentions for the creation—the 'alpha and omega'. In other words, God sees—in his mind's eye—or otherwise, the whole picture, and it is this that is 'very good'. For God, surely, sees the beginning from the end and rejoices in the fact that 'Creation' is, de facto, very good. And this de facto good is not because 'the ends justify the means' but rather that 'the means' (the process) is the only possible way for God to bring about an end that not only justifies the creator but that brings, at the eschaton, the best of possible outcome for all creatures—including God's victory over his enemies.

The philosopher Richard Swinburne is of the opinion that a perfectly good God would seek to do many good actions and no bad actions. Swinburne opines that "good actions often derive their goodness from bringing about states of affairs which are intrinsically good, that is good because of what they are and not because of how they were brought about or what they cause." (Swinburne, 1998). Understanding what is meant by goodness is crucial for the question of theodicy. Swinburne's comments are especially relevant regarding evolutionary theodicy and bear on the question of what the Bible means by 'good'. Jörgen Moltmann argued that the creation's beginnings do not define its overall potential—or indeed its 'goodness':

> The accounts of the creation-in-the-beginning do not as yet talk about creation to the glory of God. Only the Sabbath of creation is more than 'very good'. It is hallowed, sanctified and therefore points to creation's future glory. The Sabbath is, as it were, the promise of future consummation built into the initial creation. (1996)

Moltmann's comments are insightful in that he offers, here, a rationale for past events and future 'glories' but without committing himself to a true definition of 'goodness'—apart from it (creation) being, at its inception 'hallowed' and 'sanctified'. However, Moltmann's definition,will not suffice as he does not appear to align himself with any clear definition of 'the good' of creation. The question arises: Was it good or not?

The answer to this question is that 'The Creation' was 'very good'.

Herbert McCabe (2010) working from the thought of Thomas Aquinas, argues that:

> God whose essence is not potential with respect to existence, and which therefore does not constitute a limiting context for transcendental words (i.e. goodness), we can say not merely that God is good but that God is goodness or that goodness is God.

For Aquinas, to have a concept of goodness in the sense in which we have a concept would be to comprehend God. I take this to mean that God, in God's self, is the ultimate expression of goodness. Should God be the ultimate expression of goodness it follows that it requires both prudence and humility before 'exacting judgement' on man's part—a judgement brought about by disbelief—without any comprehension of God's overall plans and intentions for God's creation.

Goodness in Question

God's purposes for His creation, it is reasonable to assume, are 'good'—good, that is, as opposed to evil, wicked, corrupt, ruthless and unscrupulous—in the ethical sense 'good and not bad'.

John Swinton (2007) refers to Martin Buber who held that 'good' was the product of striving for truth and beauty: "' goodness', Buber believed, does not occur accidentally, rather; 'it emerges from intentional practices of caring about and paying attention to particular noble goals.'" It is indeed these 'noble' goals of God that we seek to comprehend. C. John Collins (2006) suggests that the goodness of creation implies that the result of God's creative endeavors were pleasing to God; God thought that the results were good. Collins concludes that "To affirm that the creation is 'good' then, is to affirm that God takes delight in it and that man at his best will do so as well. Ernest Lucas states that the meaning of the goodness in the Creation Narrative is clear from the context: "…it pleased God. It pleased him because it reflected something of himself…The fact that it pleased God also means that it was free of evil, which becomes the major cause of the absence of shalom after the [Genesis] fall." (2001).

If therefore the creation outcome pleased God, because of the efficient (tov) nature of the creation, we can conclude that the outcome is good even though this 'good' may not, presently, be fully comprehended by lesser beings. Terence Penelhum notes (1990) that in calling God 'good', one is not merely applying to God some 'general epithet of commendation', with no ancillary commitment on what he might be expected to do. He opines that "it would be vacuous to apply the concept of goodness without a fairly detailed idea of what these standards are—the standards which the speaker must regard as applying to himself.

"Theologian, Physicist and Theistic Evolutionist, John Polkinghorne (1991) suggests that the goodness referred to by the author of Genesis should be understood in terms of what Polkinghorne calls 'fruitful potentiality' rather than some kind of initial perfection. So, for Polkinghorne, there was no perfect state but only the potential for fruitfulness. This does allow for (positive) unknown (fruitful) outcomes—the kind of potential for what God may bring about at the 'eschatological finale'. However, Polkinghorne's reference to potentiality leaves in doubt any outcome that God may, somehow, bring about, through the evolutionary 'creative' process.

Rowan Williams (2000) is more explicit in his interpretation of the Genesis narrative, allowing for the fruitful eventuality of an evolutionary process. Williams suggests that Creation in the classical sense does not involve some uncritical idea of God's monarchy—rather that, "…the absolute ascribed to God in creation means that God cannot make a reality that then needs to be actively governed, subdued, bent to the divine purpose away from its natural source." According to Williams, if God creates freely, God does not need the power of a sovereign; what is, is from God. God's sovereign purpose is what the world is becoming. This fits well with the notion that God's 'bent to the divine purpose' is none other than the 'naturally selective' processes of materialistic evolution. Williams' view allows for the introduction of a lesser 'deity'—a 'god' to suit a view that seems to leave little room for the existence of the God of Scripture. Williams' view as with Polkinghorne's, seems to leave everything open to the 'mystically-sovereign-purposes' of God. Well, we can say that we know a little of what the world was and, up until the present time, 'what is has been'. Moreover, we are informed by scientific prediction as to what the world might become. However, it is the Biblical revelation that offers us a 'God's eye view' of what God has in mind for the (biological) 'by-products' of an evolutionary process. The tension here is obvious: Should the creation have been completed sometime back in the distant (or not so distant) past then there would not have been a process taking, according to current cosmological knowhow, some 13.8 billion years to complete. It would have been a 'finished' work and there would be no question of God lacking power or needing to relinquish power in order to allow for a more intimate connection with the creation process. However, the insights of Williams and Polkinghorne are helpful in that they point us to a future in which God's infinite goodness may realise vindication. However, it is not sufficient enough to philosophize about an unknown future—even when supporting the notion of the goodness of the God of Scripture. There is, surely, something more to offer for those seeking answers. The search for a plausible theodicy is, indeed, the raison d'être of this book.

PART2

Differing Perspectives

As a means of delving a little deeper into the world of theodicy this section introduces and interacts with the published works of a few from within the world of both science and philosophy, i.e. those who are engaged in the area of theodicy—of defending both the existence of God and the goodness of God—in the light of or in spite of Post Darwinian Materialism.

'Red in Tooth & Claw'

Michael Murray (2008) offers what he terms as a reasonable defence for the existence of gratuitous evils: 'a thin defence' rather than a 'thick defence'. Murray's 'defences' are composite—combinations of what Murray refers to as forms of causa dei (CD): arguments in defence of God—the hope/intention being that the combination of defences will be enough to persuade the objector as well as encouraging the believer. It is, of course, the case that the success of any defence of the problem of evil is dependent on an individual's 'warranted acceptances' or presuppositions. However, in a combination of defences, there might be, at least, one 'on offer' that is acceptable to the protagonist. Chapter 7 is a series of 'Combined CDs'. It follows that Murray is not convinced that any (one) explanation for God's allowance of the existence of gratuitous evils is sufficient but that, taken together, some of these CDs might suffice.

Murray takes an interesting excursion into the principle of Nomic Regularity, i.e. the notion of 'chaos to order' through which God was able to bring forth a 'positive end product'; the idea being that, at least partly, this Nomic Regularity (NR) is a sufficient reason for the 'developmental' necessity for animal suffering. In other words, NR (in the universe) allowed for the actual evolution of biological life-forms and that this 'lengthy' process (with all the implications for suffering and death of numerous creatures) brought about the 'greater good' of creatures such as modern man. Murray's NR is an essential feature of [theistic] evolution as it offers a 'signpost' for the existence of God. However, with regards to animal pain and suffering, Murray states that "…if justifiable at all, [it] is justified as a necessary condition for outweighing goods which either are enjoyed by creatures other than those that suffer or serve to enhance the goodness of the universe at the global level."

Murray's question—as to whether or not there could have been a better world introduces a comment from the eccentrically brilliant Woody Allen, who suggested that the worst that could be said on God's behalf is that 'he's an underachiever'. Murray himself states that a complete causa dei of this (NR) sort faces two 'insurmountable hurdles'. The first hurdle is that such an account does not seem to have the resources to explain why exactly there has to be so much pre-human animal pain and suffering. And secondly, that it is hard to see how the 'good' of free and effective choice by creatures like ourselves requires the existence of animals pre-existent to humans that have [to have] 'second-order mental states of the sort that make animal pain and suffering morally salient'. Murray's 'hurdle' is indeed difficult to assail unless the evolutionary path should have had no other means of bringing about the unswerving plans of the God who is there, and who cares deeply for all that he has made. However, the issue raised here is that of morality—God's morality—the perceived issue of 'natural evil'. Murray concludes that the theist has good reason to believe that Nomic Regularity is 'a highly desirable feature of creation' and that it does explain a variety of types of natural evil, but that the theist would not have sufficient reason to think that animal suffering would be among them. Of course, apart from this Nomic Regularity, there may never have arisen any prospect of the emergence (however temporal) of the abundant life that has appeared, over time, on this planet.

Nomic Regularity aside: because 'higher-order-thought' creatures share the same vulnerability, there might be sufficient reasons for this state of affairs—as Christopher Southgate (2008) points out when he says that this world is the only possible type of world for such creatures to arise. Of course, just because the world tends to follow rules or principles that produce an orderly system, it does not follow that the predictability of the ordered system (our world) is the kind of system an omniscient, omnipotent and benevolent mind would have 'engineered'. It may, of course, indicate the existence of an intelligent cause but that may be all it does. To argue that the existence of suffering is the result of the activity of a system that functions in a regular way is fine but it tells us nothing whatsoever of the 'deity' behind such symmetry. The use of NR may open the closed mind to the existence of God but, most likely, not to the goodness of God in the face of the 'ills of evolution'. Murray though 'spreads the net'—hoping that his (or another's) CD is able to add weight to the general work of theodicy.

Murray is aware of the extent of the problem in constructing such a defence. He writes: "Indeed, it seems quite implausible to think that an evil as widespread as the evil in question here, animal pain and suffering, could or would be explained only by appeal to one narrow range of goods that God aims to bring about through creation and that certain types of permitted evil take such explanations seriatim."

Blaming a lesser 'deity'

John Haught (2001) holds that the continuous evolution of life, from the initial protoplasm to the end of evolution (presumably the eschaton), continues to wind its autonomous way without any tangible sign of the divine agent—most certainly not that of a cosmic engineer 'tinkering' with project creation[16][17]. Haught, indeed, refers to the impressiveness of a divine maker of a 'self-creative' world and suggests that 'the divine maker of such a self-creative world is arguably much more 'impressive—hence worthier of human reverence and gratitude—than a 'designer' who molds and micro-manages everything directly[18]. Haught makes reference to the work of Paul Tillich, who held the view that nature had an inexhaustible dimension—and that this dimension allows theology to avoid what Haught refers to as 'the traps that occur whenever we wonder how God could possibly act or intervene in nature'. In answer to the question, 'What is really going on in nature?' Haught says , "…if nature has an inexhaustible depth, we can respond to this question by differentiating reading levels, such as those of science and theology, without having to resort to fruitless speculation about how divine influence somehow 'hooks itself' into natural processes." Haught's point here seems to be that there are different levels of 'interpretation' and that, to avoid

---

A possible scenario as being 'dead on delivery'. (2010, 63)

(Haught, God After Darwin: A Theology of Evolution 2001, 42)

wasting time with speculative reasoning—such as attempting to locate evidence for God's craftsmanship at the molecular level—theologians should leave science to the scientist—concentrating more on matters of theology. For Haught the important question is not how God acts in nature but how deep we are willing to look in our quest to understand 'what's really going on in the drama of life and the cosmos'. He refers to evolution as a 'still-unfinished drama rather than a factory of designs' and argues that accidents, natural selection and time are instances of the elements necessary to any dramatic story, and that focusing on evolution as a still-unfinished drama rather than a factory of designs is crucial. The question is: Where is this seemingly directionless, openly indefinable journey heading? Moreover, how is it possible for God to be responsible for the direction of the evolutionary process (in control of it in some tangible way), and therefore culpable? Haught is aware that 'most readers' of Darwin's Origin of Species would consider that a 'do-nothing God' differs little from no God at all but nevertheless describes God as, "…the inexhaustible dimension of depth beneath the surface of our lives and of nature."He goes on to suggest that this God may seem absent or even non-existent since we have no evidence of depth in the scientific sense. Darwin, in other words, has portrayed the life-story as a true adventure.

Evolution is a risk-taking and extravagantly inventive drama. Alongside its lush creativity, there always exists the possibility of tragic outcomes, including abundant suffering and perpetual perishing. Haught suggests that, to Christians, there is something 'cruciform' about the whole drama of life. There is 'something cruciform going on'—Indeed, the evolutionary process can be viewed as being 'a risk-taking and extravagantly inventive drama'. Some interpreters may wish to leave it there—'content' in their ignorance—disallowing the likelihood of God having any ultimate 'design' objective for His creation. Haught is correct of course when he claims that a 'theology of evolution' is not interested in defending the idea of a 'designer God' per se, "…as this would only make us wonder why the 'designer' does not immediately eliminate the disorder of suffering in the drama of life." In other words: why would the designer make no effort to 'immediately' eliminate the effects of the bad design—should there have been a 'bad design' in the first place. Along with Christopher Southgate and others, I do not hold the view that there ever was a 'bad design' or a malfunction within the universal law of physics—contrary to Adrian Hough's (2010) interesting idea of a 'flaw in the universe'. However, it is the case that these 'actual laws' dictate outcomes. Ergo, any changes to the physical laws may change the status quo in the creation ideal.

Regarding evolutionary theory, Haught asks whether or not 'a theology of evolution' can, indeed, make sense of 'life's suffering'. His conclusion is that it cannot, as yet do so. Moreover if there ever was a question resistant to receiving a presently satisfying response, it is that of why the drama of life involves so much agony and loss: "To make ourselves receptive to any answer at all, however, we must be prepared to wait. Such is the requirement of faith." Haught is, of course, correct—we can only speculate as we do not have all the answers.

Waiting is a requirement of faith (Hebrews Chapter 11). However, the Christian faith is based on both future revelation (what Scripture points to) and past (not too insignificant) events such as the incarnation and resurrection (what Scripture attests). Of course there are questions, scientific or otherwise that, in spite of our persistent endeavors, shall remain unanswered. Haught though, I maintain, is incorrect in his bleak analysis—as if Scripture gives no clue to the purposes of the God of creation.

The language Haught uses is contemporary, and it fits in well with current theistic-evolutionary views of craftsmanship rather than design. God's desire to produce the 'Greatest Show on Earth' (Dawkins 2009) may well be 'reason enough' for the existence of pain and suffering, but this reasoning will not suffice to defend the notion of a benevolent God. Whatever one makes of this kind of reasoning, it is not sufficient enough to 'get God off the hook'—at least not the God whose benevolent character would, according to some, not have allowed such compromise. Haught's God, though, seems not to be in danger of needing any kind of defence.

'End-Time Answers': *Waiting for the Parousia*

In the introduction of his book 'The Groaning of Creation' : God, Evolution and the Problem of Evil (Southgate, 2008)', Christopher Southgate states that species as we know them are as they are because of the pressure of natural selection and predator-prey cycles—and that, 'we can now see why pain and violence are endemic in nature.' Southgate refers to the environmental philosopher and theologian Holmes Rolston III. Rolston, who having listed the more positive aspects of the evolutionary process, stated that, "… It is also, orderly, prolific, efficient, selecting for adaptive fit, exuberant, complex, diverse, regenerating life generation after generation." In other words (m no words rather than Rolston's) there is 'meaning' and, some kind of order in evidence.

If, as Southgate suggests, death is actually a 'thermodynamic necessity', it is, indeed, difficult to imagine the biological process/system without death. We may well be dealing with a God who had but the one 'option' for his creation purposes. Southgate states that even though we can never be sure that the evolutionary process was God's only way to give rise to creatures such as stem from the 3.8 or so billion-year-long evolution of the Earth's biosphere, we can only say that, given what we know about creatures—especially what is (*presently*) known about the role of the evolutionary process in refining biological characteristics.

Moreover, the sheer length of time the process has required to give rise to sophisticated sentience—it is eminently plausible and coherent to suppose that this was the only way open to God[19].

The 'Only Way' option is a view also held by, among others, Professor R.J.Russell. (2008) Russell gives detailed reasons for holding a view that is committed to biological evolution being the only way God could have produced the present day results. Should God have had only the 'one option', through which to create a world, one could rightfully suppose that we are not dealing with an omnipotent God. Southgate, however, is not suggesting that the Triune God is anything other than omnipotent; however, it does follow that various aspects of God's 'being' might well be in question should it be that, somehow, the God of Christian belief could not have produced a better process for the Goals (Telos) of an omnipotent and omniscient God.

Southgate explores the notion of kenosis and its relevance for evolutionary theodicy and refers to the 'panentheistic' term 'deep intratrinitarian kenosis', i.e. that the 'self-abandoning love of the Father in begetting the Son establishes an otherness that enables God's creatures to be (what Southgate terms) 'selves'.

---

[19] Southgate's is a good argument as the point is that it is God's use of evolution that is in question and it is the evolutionary process that is broadly accepted. The only objection (at least from my perspective) is that it may be seen to diminish God's omnipotence—but does it?

It is, therefore, 'selving'—the self-development of biological (sentient) 'selves', i.e. the 'selving' goal of the evolutionary process that is seen by Southgate and by some other proponents as a major goal of evolution. Should there have been no such thing as evolutionary process, there would, of course, have been no possibility for any such selving to occur. Southgate proposes that the evolutionary struggle of creation can be read as being the 'travail' to which God subjected creation in the hope that the values of complex life, and ultimately freely choosing creatures such as ourselves, would emerge.' It is, of course, a possibility that unguided [Darwinian] processes would produce less than the 'hoped-for' outcomes.

Southgate reminds his readers that he is not advancing the view that the evolutionary process has been damaged by 'Adamic' fallenness. Indeed, Southgate, as with most Christian evolutionists, realizes the evident contradictions between a creation that is 'frustrated' and that 'groans (Romans 8:20-22) and a 'creation' that is the craftsmanship of a loving, caring, benevolent God. Southgate would readily concur with the view that this earthly state of affairs may be seen as a system that is in need of healing—but not from any kind of human failing per se.

Furthermore, Southgate maintains that we shall fulfil our co-redeeming role by becoming partners with God in the healing of our little corner of the cosmos when we reveal our true Christ-likeness by having our minds set on servanthood.

Moreover, we shall transcend ourselves not by the consummation of all our desires but through re-educating them with wisdom, so as to liberate the nonhuman creation from this particular mark of its travail. It is Southgate's contention that this renewing of the mind' produces the necessary 'self-giving'—a self-giving (love) that emanates from the relationship within the Trinity. However, it is, surely the 'human animal', rather than any other species, that fares best out of the evolutionary environment. Southgate highlights the fact that the human animal has access to an extent of freedom and self-transcendence that goes vastly beyond what is present to other animals. However, that 'potentiality' is not an absolute—humanity has the potential for both good and evil. Indeed, mankind may be, through the evolutionary process, [becoming] something 'ignoble' rather than something 'noble'; bearing the imago Dei does not guarantee good choices, as both the Scriptures and the evidence of history confirm. Of course, for those in Christ the potential to bring about change is, indeed, enormous; but this is, mostly, a potentiality to be fully realized rather than an actuality. Whatever it is that God intends for humanity or other creatures (at some point in the future) the facts are that the death of all creatures, according to Natural Selection, fuels evolutionary processes leading to the demise of the weak and the survival of the better-equipped predator. Despite predation (before the appearance of modern-man) there would have existed a prolific, 'self-sustaining', abundant, diverse, creation. Death though can be seen as the final victor unless, somehow, God redeems the 'unfairness' and brings about whatever can be believed to be 'greater goods' for the recipients of the unjust treatment meted out by the evolutionary process.

Southgate argues that a scientifically informed eschatology 'must' try and give some sort of account of what might be continuities and discontinuities between this creation and the new one. Any such 'future hope' though does not depend on our present understanding of just how this universe (any parallel universes) or how any new planetary systems function, but on that which God has promised in Scripture.

Vital to the ojectives of Southgates' book is his conviction that scientifically informed eschatology must also attempt to relate to the final transforming act of God of which the resurrection of Christ is usually regarded as the beginning of such a transformational epoch[20]. Southgate, along with Michael Murray, offers an amalgam of defences—the core of which (listed a-e) are as follows:

a) That the goodness of creation gives rise to all sorts of values.
b) That pain, suffering, death, and extinction are intrinsic to a creation evolving according to Darwinian principles.
c) That an evolving creation was the only way, God could

---

[20] This is not just regarding continuities and discontinuities in human life but also to our understanding of God's relation to living creatures other than human beings.

produce all the 'beauty, diversity, sentience, and sophistication that the biosphere exhibits.

d) That God co-suffers with every sentient being in creation.

e) That the Cross of Christ is 'the epitome' of divine compassion, God's assuming of ultimate responsibility for the pain of creation—the Cross inaugurating the transformation of creation (the ending of the groaning Paul refers to in Romans 8:22)

According to Southgate, the importance of giving an account of how such a loving God (of loving relationship) must provide an eschatological fulfilment for creatures that have no flourishing in this life, i.e. that God could never regard such a creature as 'a mere evolutionary expedient', is paramount. Southgate opines that, if divine fellowship with creatures such as us is, in any sense a goal of evolutionary creation, this 'may' lead to the possibility that humans have a crucial and positive role, cooperating with their God in the healing of the evolutionary process—the 'co-redeemer' argument.

NB. Southgate does not differentiate between any notions of 'redeemed humanity' or otherwise; but seems to be referring to humankind in general.[21]

---

[21] Evolution though is, from the position of the argument in this book, not something that is broken—rather it is this way for a reason—and God has subjected the creation to this system so that God, in Christ, could redeem all that

That creation engenders many sorts of values is, without doubt, the case. Moreover, that an evolving creation was necessary for God's purposes is accepted as a 'given' in the majority of theistic evolutionary circles—a de facto, even necessary, state of affairs. Southgate's argument that God co-suffers with every sentient being is plausible, as this would be a necessary expression of the compassion of the God of the Bible. However, I suggest that God as 'co-sufferer' does not indicate culpability on God's part but rather speaks of empathetic solidarity of God with his creatures. It is agreed that some kind of 'eschatological fulfilment' for creatures that have 'no flourishing in this life' shall (somehow) pertain— though 'we' have no idea how this would 'pertain'. It is hard to imagine a world without entropic consequences—at least not a similar world to this in which the same physical laws prevail. Southgate's view that humans have a positive cooperative role with God in the healing of the evolutionary process is interesting. It is the case that, in the twenty-first century, humankind has both the means (technologically) and, to a lesser extent, the will (morally & ethically) to address the prevailing state of affairs. Southgate's suggestions, though interesting, cannot be of major significance in terms of the creation of <u>God's promise</u> of a New

which is broken and transform it. Indeed, this is the only means through which God could resolve the problem of moral evil and to release the creation from its bondage.

Heaven and the 'New' Earth[22]. It is, one might suggest, entirely possible that at the eschaton, God may 'release' those transformed into Christ's likeness into the work of redeeming this amazing world. Furthermore, one may assume that, 'Post Eschaton', the 'New Humanity' will be equipped with far greater knowledge and wherewithal to bring about the changes that our world awaits. It is, most, likely, that to which Paul refers in Romans chapter 8. These 'sons of God' shall be, one assumes, like that of the resurrection body of Christ. Soli Deo Gloria.

Obscuring Beginnings:

Karl Barth and Nature

Evolutionary theory has exacerbated the problem of natural evil for the believer—leaving the existence of benevolence within the character of the Godhead questionable. Darwinian Natural Selection has, without doubt, greatly diminished the likelihood of there being a satisfactory outcome in the work of theodicy. Neil Messer, however, offers a possible way ahead.

---

[22] However, it was, indeed, God's intention regarding the people of Israel (C. Wright 2006) and that it continues to be God's intention regarding those professing to follow Christ in the 'latter days'.—not, particularly regarding the 'functional' role that some commentators assign to mankind (i.e. imago Dei)—but that Christian profession is not less than 'confessional'—but that being the people of God has other implications that will not allow for excuses or indeed for lethargy or complacency. Indeed, I am reminded of the Parable of the Talents (Matthew 25:14-30).

At the beginning of his chapter in the edited book 'Theology after Darwin' (Messer, N., 2009), Messer outlines his intended course—stating that a more satisfactory approach to the problem of evolutionary evil is to be taken from the perspective of Christian tradition rather than from any scientific interpretation or overview. Messer, a scientist and a theologian, also refers to his approach and that it is developed in dialogue with the twentieth-century Swiss theologian Karl Barth. Messer refers to 'Mapping the Problem of Evolutionary Evil'—making reference to two strands: the stronger strand advocates that the evolutionary process is the means that God used to 'create' all biological life. The weaker claim is that which applies to 'the conviction that the world which God made and pronounced 'very good' (Genesis 1:31) is a world that has a process of evolution by natural selection built into it'. Messer suggests that one obstacle that modern biology 'seems' to place in the way of both the weak and strong claims is that the evolutionary process inevitably entails 'ills' or 'evils', i.e. the pain and death of all creatures. It is this 'inevitability' factor that poses the problem—markedly within the world of evolutionary theodicy.

Messer offers an alternative approach to the problem and refers to two aspects of approaches to the problem of evil. Firstly he refers to the apparent contradiction between the world disclosed to us by evolutionary biology and the creation that God (Genesis 1:31) pronounces 'very good'. Secondly, he refers to the more familiar question of whether an omnipotent God could have avoided some of the evil that we find in the world.

Regarding the latter Messer states that there is a danger that if Christians pursue this line of thought too far, 'they will find themselves defending an idol of their own making rather than the God of Christian revelation.' Messer's view is taken to mean (at least by this author) that: taking such a route often leads to dead-ends or an adventure in metaphysical gymnastics rather than an adequate theodicy. Messer's point, as viewed here, is that any 'enquiry' of this sort needs to start with the Christian community's confession of faith in response to the biblical witness. Messer is fully aware of the problems and lists the major difficulties:

a) That the Scriptures witness to a God who created all that is, and who pronounced the creation 'very good' (Genesis 1:31)

b) That the Genesis creation narratives and other biblical texts flesh out what we are to understand by 'very good', 'a world of peace and plenty.' Messer states that if in any sense, the Christian doctrine of creation and Darwinian evolutionary biology are referring to the same world then we seem to be faced with a contradiction.

I take it that the 'contradiction' Messer refers to in 'b' is that the God of the Bible would not have devised such a system as the one in question and then declared it 'very good'. Messer is partly right in that God would not have created such a world as normally attributed to 'Darwinian Natural Selection'. However, in spite of what Messer feels to be a contradiction, it is possible to affirm—along with Scripture: that the creation was 'excellent', in the sense of it being fit for purpose—or as Polkinghorne (1991) suggests: it was good because it had 'fruitful potentiality'. The view held here, though, is that any notion of 'potentiality' must take into consideration God's sovereign purposes—the purposes of a God who has the wherewithal to bring about an ultimate telos. This notion is in stark contrast to a God who has no means of bringing about His plans and purposes i.e. a 'god' who does not know the end from the beginning—or vis versa. Christopher Southgate's response to Messer is that Messer is simply unwilling to concede that the disvalues we see in evolution could be part of God's creation. Southgate suggests that it seems that in order to retain belief in 'the unequivocal goodness of God's creation', Messer wants to draw instead on Barth's 'Church Dogmatics' in which Barth reflects on this concept of 'nothingness'.

Regarding 'beginnings', Messer seems to be following Barth and others when he states that there never was a 'golden age'—never an idyllic period on earth when there was no predation, parasitism or plague. 'The first man was immediately the first sinner' [Barth,1956]. According to Messer, Barth is saying that history begins with the Fall—that 'the history of the world' has always been a 'fallen history'. However, this does not mean that the story of creation can be contradicted by the [so] different history supplied by evolutionary biology. Messer points out that Barth is not attempting an explanation of the origins of evil but that Barth is more interested in what God has done about the problem. This is all very well, but it seems (on the surface at least) to rather 'muddy the waters'.

'Barth', Messer states, identifies evil as 'nothingness' (das Nichtige). As such 'nothingness' has a strange, paradoxical, negative kind of existence: it is the chaos, disorder and annihilation that threatens God's creation—a threat to which God is opposed. Sin is one form that 'nothingness' takes, but it also takes the forms of suffering and death. Furthermore, it is clear that not only humanity but the whole of God's creation is threatened and opposed by this 'nothingness'. Whatever, within the evolutionary process, is opposed to God's creative purpose is to be identified with 'nothingness': it is an aspect of the chaos and disorder threatening the creation.

Messer affirms that the Biblical witness requires us to say of the world: that it is both created and fallen, that creation is the work of God, that it was pronounced 'very good', and that it is badly astray from what God means it to be[23]. In contradistinction to Messer's view, my view is that creation, in terms of God's

---

[23] It's interesting to note that Messer (2009, 150) thinks that there could be closer links than we sometimes think between the violence of the struggle for existence and—at least some aspects of human sin. I agree with this—it is so much more than we see or even perceive.

planned intentions, is (though it is impossible to qualify because of the unverifiable effects of the behaviour of fallen angels) as God intended i.e. that creation has an evolutionary 'blueprint' because of the planned intentions of the God who is: omniscient,benevolent and sovereign[24]. Messer aligns himself with an evolutionary perspective and states that it is the evolutionary process that has made us the way we are. However, he follows Barth in identifying the violence and scarcity of the struggle for existence with what he considers 'the fallenness of the world'. The argument in this book though is that there is, indeed, a fallenness but that the cause of that fallenness need not remain unexamined, i.e. an 'unknown cause' or an 'abstract form'—a das Nichtige that leaves aside the need for an answer to the problem of evil. The argument in this essay is that the fallenness, of angels and of men—though not instigated by God was, somehow, known by God before the creation of this universe. For this world is the best possible world in which the Triune God brings about the best of possible outcomes. Messer, however, is concerned not to blur the edges— making God's good creative purpose and the flawed evolutionary process into two co-eternal powers vying for the upper hand in shaping us.' Neither is Messer wishing to re-invent a form of Manichaeism, in which light battles darkness or any form of

---

[24] This is not to say that created agents have not brought about states of affairs that may be considered a contradiction, regarding God's attributes of benevolence and sovereignty, but that it is nothing of the sort.

Gnosticism[25]—where the material world is irretrievably flawed and salvation lies in escaping from it. The reason we do not have to do either of these things, Messer suggests, is because God has, in Christ, addressed our predicament.

According to Messer, Barth held that in the incarnation God exposed Himself to nothingness—doing so in order to repel and defeat it. He adds to this by referring to Paul's words in 1 Corinthians 15:3-4 where the apostle states that, "Christ died for our sins in accordance with the scriptures, and that he was buried, and that he was raised from the dead on the third day in accordance with the scriptures." Messer affirms that:

> Because this is the heart of the [Christian] good news, Gnosticism is not an option: the Christian gospel promises not an escape from the material but its healing and transformation…The Christian tradition understands the resurrection of Christ as the in-breaking of God's promised new age into history, the first fruits of what God promises to do to 'make all things new'. Revelation 21:5.

It is, as Messer suggests, the 'transformation' that is the good news. However, should there be any need of 'healing' the inference would be that the creation is out of sorts with its creator

---

[25] Neither is this the view in the argument in this book—in which neither Dualism (Gnostic or otherwise) or any other proposed opposition to the sovereign will of God could obtain.

or that another party/parties had ruined the ideal. Messer admits that the kind of world to which "a wolf hath sojourned with a lamb, And a leopard with a kid doth lie down, And calf, and young lion, and fatling are together, And a little youth is leader over them." [26]is beyond our [present] comprehension especially in the light of evolutionary biological outcomes. However, because of Messer's high view of biblical revelation and his insistence that theological interpretation takes precedence over any scientifically derived a priori—this is his position. Messer is surely correct in this—for it is the 'theological' that is in question and not, at present, the 'scientific'. Messer affirms what is the Christian hope: that God's peace, not the struggle for existence, will have the last word—and because God's 'good future' has broken into our [present] with the resurrection of Christ, we are able to see 'the past and the beginning' in a true light as well.

In the final part of his discourse Messer admits that his 'picture' does not offer much by way of explanation—of how the struggle for existence came to be such a pervasive feature of our present reality. He does suggest, however, that the important question to report is what God has done to address our predicament and our response to God's solution. Messer's is a familiar voice. Reaching into the eschaton for consolation may well be preferable to wallowing in the [muddy] waters of the 'dim' past, but this in and of itself does not match up to an adequate defence, let alone a

---

[26] Isaiah 11:6-9

theodicy. However, Messer's commitment to the prioritising of the revelation of God (in Scripture) over the, present, conclusions of mankind 'the latter-day fruit of evolution' is one readily concurred with. Indeed, it is because of the revelation of Scripture—declaring the omnipotence and benevolence of God—that the problem arises otherwise there is no such problem.

Although Messer's Barthian defence—in its apparent attempt to avoid any prehistorical conjecture—focusing instead on the future hope that Scripture promises at the eschaton—is comforting, it does nothing to address the 'why question', but rather consigns the problem to mystery that is Barth's nothingness' (das Nichtige).The problem though is too significant to relegate to such an unknown—unknowable past. There is, I shall argue, a far better defence—a defence that has an 'alpha and omega' factor.

Against Instrumentalism:

Cause & Effect

Michael Lloyd (2018), along with Neil Messer, realizes that the problem of an evolutionary defence, let alone a convincing theodicy, is acute for the Christian defender as it entails dealing with the contradictions of a world in which the 'love of God' is [has not been] altogether evident. Lloyd states that:

> You only have to look at the natural world (or look at documentary programs about the natural world) to see that

it is riddled with pain, death, disease, and predation. And a moment's reflection will further reveal that these are not incidental to creation but appear to be built into its very fabric…

Writing in 'Are Animals Fallen? (1998), Lloyd points out that this world is certainly not the sort of world which one would expect the God we meet in Christ to have created. Lloyd writes that the protest against, what he refers to as, 'the predatory character of nature' is precisely because of the Christological conception of God held by Christians. It is though far broader than any underdeveloped Christology, for, it is the very idea of the 'Sovereign God' (The Triune God of Scripture) that is in question. In other words, the life and teachings of the incarnate son of God cannot be taken in isolation from the actual telos of the Triune God—a telos that has to do with justice as well as redemption—with judgement as well as reconciliation.

Regarding the defence offered by instrumentalists (that God will bring good out of harms and that the harms are a necessary part of the 'plot'),Lloyd comments that, "…even without pain, predation does not seem unambiguously to declare the glory of God, and theodicies which seek to justify predation as part of the creational purposes of God tend to adopt anti-Christian attitudes in the attempt." Lloyd further points out that with an instrumentalist view of evolution God is responsible for the suffering involved, but not culpable, because God is using it as an instrument in the pursuit of some greater good, be it aesthetic richness or human freedom. Lloyd though says that 'Eschatology' by itself is not sufficient however great the happiness, peace and rest on offer these alone do not justify the means, and that the problem must be addressed at the other end as well. Lloyd argues that what is needed is an account of evil in which God is not only victoriously against it at the end but is also resolutely against it at the beginning. In other words, we need a doctrine of The Fall as well as an end-times solution. I affirm Lloyd's view—vis a vis the need for a comprehensive defence that takes into account all the necessary ingredients—but arrive at a somewhat different conclusion on the matter. Lloyd is convinced that the only possible defence for God against the charge of making a world riddled with suffering and violence is that God did not: "And that is what the doctrine of The Fall tells us." Lloyd's view sees The Fall as cosmic and not local, and that it is not limited to human sin. Lloyd's view also sees that animals are part of a fallen creation and therefore subject to its state of affairs. He notes that those who hold to the fallenness of the whole of creation do so not primarily to 'get faith out of an apologetic hole', but for intrinsic theological and Christological reasons which they see embedded in the revelation of God in Christ and Scripture. Lloyd though states that since the arrival of Darwinism the effects of the human fall could no longer be taken as the cause of predation and death and suggested that the question had to be faced as to how, that which was ill-disposed to the creational intention of an omnipotent God, could have come to be:

> Granted that the whole of creation is fallen, how did it fall?
> Granted that the divisions of creation are not a design fault
> of the Creator but the result of free decisions by free
> creatures, what account may we give of the volitional
> process or processes which brought about the Fall?

Interestingly, Lloyd refers to the work of the twentieth century theologian N.P.Williams (1998) who rejected the idea that humans were 'the ultimate culprits' for all of the ills within the evolutionary scheme of things but, nevertheless, insisted that the Fall must have taken place in time as any attempt to lift the ultimate origin of evil out of time would plunge us into the gulf of either dualism or of unmoral monism.

'Unmoral Monism' I consider to be one of the greatest challenges to Twenty First Century Christian Belief

Lloyd himself prefers to work with a model of The Fall that is angelic in origin. He suggests that, the hypothetical assertion that natural evil is the result of the distortion of creation brought about by the angelic fall, does not need evidential support at this precise point, if it can be shown that it is organically related to a world-view which is coherent and carries evidential support at other key points[27] i.e. that, 'The doctrine of the Fall implies that creation is

---

[27] Lloyd refers to past theories related to the existence of objects in the universe that were later proven to be factual.

fallen, that it does not reflect the self-giving love of God that we meet in Christ, and that the God we do meet in Christ is the sort of God who gives creatures that freedom to reject God's purposes without which love is meaningless; if we understand 'godless' to mean 'having turned away from God.' Indeed, I concur with Llloyd that, the expressive free will of both angels and men are at the root of the problem of moral evil—the effects of which are, as yet, not fully comprehended.

As Lloyd has stated, and as is agreed with here; Free Will is a necessary part of the outworking of God's creative purposes. If this is the case then there must be some cause and effect resulting from free will decisions. However, as Southgate points out, "…a position such as Lloyd's still suffers from the problem…that it dissects out the biological world and assigns all the disvalue to the free (harmful) choices of angels, and all the values to God's creative work." (Robinson & Southgate, 2011) Southgate is, in my opinion, correct in his assessment of Lloyd's '1998' work but Southgate's view is not the final word on the viability of a Free-Will Defence, neither is it the 'final word' on the idea of there being anything other than 'Natural Selection' with the 'wherewithal' to affect change within the 'created order'.

And then there are the deleterious effects of humankind's alleged 'progress' on the created order.

Irenaeus & Augustine:

Differing Perspectives

The physicist and theologian Robert J. Russell has done much to set out a conceptual framework for considering the problem of evolutionary theodicy. Russell draws heavily on the work of Irenaeus as he develops his defence of the goodness of God in the light of evolution. Russell proposes that any 'robust theodicy' has to meet at least three criteria:

1. It must ward off Manichean tendencies to "blame a lesser God" for creating natural evil,or to view nature as unambiguously evil,
2. It must ward off Pelagian tendencies to undercut the universality of moral evil,
3. It must fully take on board [Darwinian] evolution, and in particular the constitutive character of natural evil to life.

Russell notes that Christian theology includes a variety of theodicies (defences) that meet these criteria, and refers to John Hick's analysis of this variety as falling into two broad types—the Augustinian and Irenaean; Russell then endeavors to reformulate these theodicies so that they meet all three criteria—deploying them to the task of evolutionary theodicy. Russell offers some cautionary comments and interesting insights regarding Augustine's 'Free Will Defence' and suggests that, for Augustine, both natural and moral evils are 'ultimately' the result of the actions of free rational beings who sin. Augustine's view was that sin began with the cosmic fall of the angels and continued with Adam and Eve who, though created 'very good' by God, did of their own free will choose creaturely goods over God.

Extending the Augustinian theodicy to physics and cosmology Russell suggests that there are resources in an Augustinian theodicy which should not be overlooked. Russell refers to the work of Reinhold Niebuhr who suggests that the first task required (in order to divest the Augustinian theodicy of its 'creation/fall' framework) was to uncover its underlying philosophical argument and then to reinterpret this argument in/with an evolutionary perspective. Niebuhr then rendered the underlying logic of the Augustinian theodicy as asserting that sin is unnecessary but inevitable. This phrase, according to Russell, captures Augustine's argument without tying it to the Fall. It expresses in stark terms what Niebuhr called the 'absurd paradox' of the Christian free-will defence. This is, I suggest, a mistake as it does not take into consideration the potential for both good and evil that God has allowed within the created order—so does not allow for a more comprehensive free-will argument.

Under the heading: 'Preconditions in physics that underlie the free-will defence' Russell asks, what, in particular, must physics be like for the reformulated Augustinian/Niebuhrian free-will defence to hold. Moreover, what, if anything, reflects the Niebuhrian logic of 'unnecessary but inevitable' at the level of physics? Russell refers to thermodynamics—and the work of what he terms 'metaphorical theology' summarizing the views of its exponents thus:

> To summarize the idea briefly, we typically find beauty and goodness in the patterns of emergent complexity and creative novelty characteristic of life, while tragedy and sorrow play themselves out in terms of the dissipation and destruction associated with decay, disease and death. Curiously, thermodynamics underlies and is entailed by all these phenomena. The second law [of thermodynamics] thus plays a dual role: It makes possible the physical and biological consequences of our moral action both for good and for ill. (2008)

The unavoidable conclusion of Niebuhrian logic seems to be that sin (deviant behaviour, disobedience etc.) is the de facto result of the system through which God has created life-forms—including sentient beings such as 'Adam and Eve'. The question becomes, as Russell underlines: "Why did God choose to create this universe with these laws of physics knowing that they would not only make Darwinian evolution unavoidable[28], and with it the sweep of natural evil in the biological realm, but that they would also contribute to natural evil at the level of physics...." Russell's conclusion on the matter is that the 'Augustinian/ Niebuhrian

---

[28] The assumption here is that, as materialists assert, the evolutionary process was inevitable. This, of course, is not a scientifically verifiable notion.

theodicy (ultimately) fails. So, why does it fail? It fails, according to Russell, not because it is tied to a 'mythical fall' because it is not. Neither is its failure due to its mistaking death as a consequence of 'sin' and not as constitutive of life. It avoids both admirably. According to Russell, it leads to the (unhelpful) recognition that, 'underlying moral evil is natural evil' and that this recognition (conclusion) characterizes the universe as a whole. As according to Russell et al.: 'Evil' is intrinsic to the processes that generate value. NB. Russell's position: that, due to the physics, there exists an unavoidable state of affairs such as 'natural selection' suggests: any notion of a telos for God to aspire to is somewhat of an oxymoron—I shall argue that this is surely not the case. However, I agree with Russell when he states that the cause of evil is moral rather than natural—though this may be a question of differing interpretations. It is the case that [should] the laws of physics functioned to different values there might well be no likelihood of the entropic effects of the Second Law of Thermodynamics; thus, in such a world, there may not be the physical means through which the results of rebellious malevolence could manifest itself. Natural evil may (paradoxically) exist as a result of moral deviancy but, as is argued elsewhere in this book: This world is the only possible world in which the second person of the Trinity could take on flesh, suffer and die—in so doing rescue, ransom and redeem a creation that 'groans'—in the waiting. Russell, meanwhile, looks to the redemption of the cosmos, which may be seen as an eschatological 'get-out-of-jail' card.

Russell returns to the work of John Hick—'retrieving and extending' Hick's ideas—commenting on what he refers to as Hick's helpful comparison of both contrasts and agreements between the theodicies of Augustine and Schleiermacher (the latter deriving some of its inspiration from Irenaeus). The essence of the difference between these theodicies, according to Russell's interpretation of Hick's views, is as follows:

> The Augustinian theodicy looks at a created paradise in the past and focuses crucial importance on the fall of angels and humankind—looking to a future of judgement for 'the damned'.

> The Irenaean theodicy accepts evil as an inevitable factor in the world—suited for moral development. It does not deny The Fall, but rejects the ideas of 'lost righteousness and inherited sinfulness'. It views an eternal hell as 'rendering a Christian theodicy impossible'.

Russell states that the key difference, as he reads Hick, is that the Augustinian theodicy attempts to protect God from responsibility for the existence of evil by stressing the Fall (Adamic & Angelic), whereas the Irenaean theodicy accepts God's ultimate responsibility for evil while 'showing' why a world that includes evil can be considered justifiable and inevitable: For the Augustinian theodicy, the world is 'very good' as it is now, even including the reality of sin and evil. For the Irenaean theodicy, the perfection of the world lies in the eschatological future where the end, the Kingdom of God, will justify the means of its achievement…The Augustinian theodicy admits that bringing good out of evil is better than not permitting evil to exist…Irenaean Theodicy treats it as central and stresses the eschatological context of the 'greater good'.

Russell concludes that 'the end is a means to the beginnings'—that God will bring an ideal end-times solution—that all will be well, so there is no need to search for an elusive answer for the state of affairs—is less than satisfactory. His explanation for the state of affairs within the created order seems to be reasonably plausible, but at the same time, it does not seem to offer anywhere near to a complete account of the extent of evil in the world. Moreover, in order to avoid any 'fall confusion,' it tempts one to engage in an eschatological 'just-so story'—and at the same time avoiding contact with the problem of evil per se. Conversely, my argument sets out to offer a defence that agrees and encompasses much of what has been said previously—but that offers a different conclusion. Russell's views fit snuggly with a 'theistic-evolutionary' view of the origins and evolution of the biosphere and avoids getting 'tied down' to 'fall narratives' of any kind. However, it will not suffice as an argument—as it is, in my opinion, de facto, not an argument.

Evolution: 'God's Response to Rebellion'

In his book entitled 'The End of Christianity: Finding a Good God in an Evil World' William Dembski makes much of the attributes of God and rails against any attempts to restrict God's activity to the metaphysical, the biophysical or 'the present tense'. Dembski asks why it is that, in the economy of the world whose creator is 'omnipotent, omniscient, and trans-temporal', should causes always precede effects? 'Clearly, such a Creator could act to anticipate events that have yet to happen. Moreover, those events could be the occasion (or cause) of God's prior anticipatory action.

Dembski takes the Adamic Fall as a significant event in the history of the world and offers a defence based on what is referred to as the 'Fall Narrative' in Genesis chapter three. Dembski refers to Adam and Eve as the initial pair of humans—as the progenitors of the whole human race; he furthermore suggests that they were specially created by God, and thus that they were not, most likely, (entirely) the result of an evolutionary process from primate or hominid ancestors. I agree with Dembski here: that there had to be an intervention—an unseen and, as yet, an undetectable 'dynamic' taking occurring in which the birth of the imago Dei (Adam & Eve) takes place. The actual detail of this, presently, lies in the somewhat speculative hands of philosophical theology rather than of science—though conjecture from both fields continues to create 'opinion' as to how it might have been 'possible' for an omnipotent deity to create something out of what (otherwise) might be considered 'natural processes'.

Dembski states that in arguing that the fall of humankind marks the entry of all evil into the world (both personal and natural evil) he makes no assumptions about the age of the Earth, the extent of evolution, or the prevalence of design. He does though state that the theodicy he develops, "…looks not to science but to the metaphysics of divine action and purpose." In other words, his concern is to offer a defence without particular deference to scientific opinion. This is an opinion with which I am in agreement. And— although, an evolutionary perspective is taken seriously, it is not allowed to dictate terms because the problem of evil, at least within the 'theistic paradigm', is not with the science but with the notion of 'Goodness' in the Divine Nature.

Dembski makes clear that the theodicy he is proposes gladly acknowledges that important similarities exist between humans and primates but, nevertheless insists that far-reaching differences also exist, "…especially differences in cognitive and moral capacities and that these represent a difference in kind and not, as Neo-Darwinists and many 'contemporary evolutionists' hold, merely a difference in degree."

Dembski's approach is one that maintains the uniqueness of the imago Dei underscoring the notion that there is indeed something uniquely significant about the 'arrival' of early humans.

Here, I am in full agreement with Dembski. Dembski, though, addresses the problem of evil with a novel alternative to the traditional offerings. His major thrust is to do with what he terms 'retroactivity': "In contrast to theodicies that attempt to justify God's goodness by limiting God, I'm going to argue that full divine foreknowledge of future contingent propositions in fact helps to reconcile God's goodness with the existence of evil. By taking a retroactive approach to the Fall, which traces all evil in the world back to human sin (even the natural evil that predates human sin), the theodicy I develop preserves the traditional view that natural evil is a consequence of the Fall." (Dembski, 2009)[29]

In essence, what Dembski proposes is that God, having observed (in Cronos time) the rebellion of the man and woman, in the perfect environment of the Garden in Eden, brought into being (in Kairos time, i.e. God's time) an evolutionary program of 'life, predation, parasitism, disease and death', as punishment for the disobedience of Adam and Eve. It was a kind of pre-emptive strike against the 'future' free-will behaviour of the Adamic pair. The traditional notion, that it was due to the [Adamic] Fall that the world became a less than the best of possible environments is, as far as I am concerned eminently defendable—especially with

---

[29]Dembski points out that a retroactive view of the fall was one of several (Christian) options proposed in the nineteenth century to explain pre-human suffering and death; Dembski refers as such to J. Dana (writing in 1853—prior to the Darwinian revolution).

Dembski's 'spin on the story'—though there are strong objections from more than a few theologians—from theologians holding an evolutionary view of the creation and those holding to a non-evolutionary view. The notion that, besides the 'fall in the garden', there should have been a more, universally (miasmatic) contaminating rebellion (though not a part of Dembski's argument) is nevertheless an essential part of the argument in this book—a Fall that brought with it globally destructive potentiality.

Dembski consistently upholds the conservative evangelical argument regarding both the 'punishment' and the 'acquittal' as well as the consequential effects on God's 'good' creation—at least when it comes to the events prior to God's 'retro-proactivity': "Thus, just as the death and resurrection of Christ is responsible for the salvation of repentant people[30] throughout all time, so the Fall of humanity in the Garden of Eden is responsible for every natural evil throughout all time (Future, present, past, and distant past preceding the Fall)." I agree with Dembski with regards to the effects of the salvific power of the cross of Christ across time. With regards to Dembski's view that the Adamic fall brought about such a kairologically 'earth-shattering' change to the order of creation, while offering affirmation here, I shall offer comments in the concluding part of this book. The question is, whether or not the course of action that Dembski suggests could be justified on

[30] Dembski offers no explicit justification for the plight of animals—or indeed the 'created order' other than human beings.

behalf of an all-knowing, all-caring omnibenevolent deity.Could the God of the Judaeo/ Christian Scriptures have brought about such a drastic state of affairs—over the disobedience of a pair of gardeners?

In offering his innovative approach Dembski allows for God to be God, and does allow 'space' for biological evolution—its cycle of life, predation and death—and this without having to deal with the notion of there being no physical death before the disobedience of advanced hominids—whenever the incident may have occurred in the space/time continuum. Dembski's approach, though dismissed by those committed to a materialist view of the evolutionary process and by those who may see it as innovative and intriguing but without much substance, are missing an opportunity to delve deeper. Dembski's view does offer a picture of God as being taken up with anger and disappointment—to the point that God brings about a retroactive state of affairs which, from an (emotionally charged) outside observer's' perspective, might seem to be an entirely unnecessary response to rebellion. Indeed, Dembski imagines a state of affairs that culminates in the punishment of creatures for a sin that had not even occurred. Dembski's thesis offers a God who punishes, seemingly innocent, creatures because of something that would occur 'long after' their having to be recipients of the effects of the second law of thermodynamics: predation, parasitism and plague; and for creatures with sufficient sentience—the experience of pain.

Dembski's thesis, indeed, seems to offer a God who punishes innocent creatures because of events beyond their control or responsibility—but there is more to a theodicy than apportioning blame entirely at the 'throne of God'.

Beyond 'pure' Darwinism

Most, 'Post-Darwin,' attempts at a defence or theodicy, avoid any notion of the prevailing state of affairs being the result of any major shift in the order of creation. Few, if any, offer an Adamic Fall as the reason for the existence of predation, plague and parasitism though some offer an Angelic Fall as an alternative—a fall that brought about and continues to bring about major negative effects on the Creation—effects that God is not responsible for, but that He allows. The majority of these defences/theodicies adhere to a theistic-evolutionary perspective—William Dembski's 'The End of Christianity' being an exception/variation.

This section interacts particularly with the views of Stephen H. Webb—as given in his book entitled (2010). Webb's view is that evolution works under divine permission and that the emergence of Humankind has particular significance within an evolutionary paradigm[31]. Webb notes that evolution leaves a trail

---

[31] Although Webb's view, that this world is NOT the best of possible worlds, is at odds with the argument given elsewhere in this book, Webb's views are nonetheless helpful regarding the development of the ideas contained within its pages.

in history—marked by blood and anguish. However, what Webb avoids saying here is that it is this very 'trail of blood and anguish' (made possible by the natural laws) that the Triune God 'commissioned' and ordained.

Along with Webb's own views I maintain that it is this very state of affairs that allows for the victory of God over both sin and death. Indeed, the song the faithful will sing and that the creation will echo is that of the Victory of God over sin and death; it will be a continual song declaring the gracious mercy and goodness of the Godhead[32]. It is this world (a world ordained and created by God) that is the only possible world—in which the free will of conscious beings can pertain with all of the resultant consequences and, most importantly, the redemptive act of the crucified son of God could possibly take place. I concur with Webb's views on the 'emergence' of humankind as being a significant 'event' in, what can be described as, the physical evolution of carbon-based life-forms: Conscious, intelligent, incredibly creative, morally aware and, most importantly, 'God Conscious'. Webb's views coalesce with the argument given in this book, i.e. that God [incarnate], at the eschaton, would dwell with a redeemed creation having rescued and redeemed the creation from its bondage to corruption.

---

[32] Donald Macleod (2000), referring to the work of B.B. Warfield says that the revelation of the trinity was made not in word but in 'deed': "It was made in the incarnation of God the Son, and the outpouring of God the Holy Spirit...the revelation of the Trinity was incidental to, and the inevitable effect of, the accomplishment of redemption."

The question of the whereabouts of this redeemed world: This 'New Heaven & New Earth, in which physical laws have a different outcome, is presently, unknown. Yet we may assume—indeed more than assume—that in the light of the promises of God there shall be a 'life-experience' for the redeemed creation in which there shall be no more plague, predation, parasitism or indeed pain, for as Scripture attests, 'the former things [shall] have passed away.' (Revelation 21:5).

This 'future world' however cannot surely be the world in which the present physical laws obtain—it is another world yet to be revealed. Yet this present world is, and has always been, a 'Necessary World'. 'Humankind' (imago Dei) is meant to be here. The 'arrival' of humans has been a major part of God's 'creation project'. I hasten to add that the argument in this book does not devalue the rest of creation or suppose that God has little more than a utilitarian purpose for it—but that this world is the way it is—not as the result of natural processes alone but as the result of the 'Telos of God'. For the God of the Judeo/Christian Scriptures is: Benevolent, Omnipotent and, indeed, Omniscient.

Robert. J. Russell advocates that the suffering of creatures cannot 'alone' be justified by the evolution of Homo sapiens and their destiny with God:

Instead, the suffering of creatures is taken up individually by God in the incarnation, suffered by God in the crucifixion, and redeemed by God in the Resurrection. This eschatological act of God is to be seen as proleptically present to and with each creature at its death.(2012)

Russell's view may be considered speculative but it is nevertheless plausible. Indeed, the effects of the Cross of Christ need to be viewed in proleptic terms—as it is in Christ's life, death and resurrection that we have sight of the 'big picture'. However, as is argued elsewhere, there needs to be an argument that addresses the origin of evil— God's reason for allowing it to remain within the created order. And, most importantly, an affirmation of God's attributes, i.e. God's Benevolence as associated with God's Omniscience and Omnipotence.

Webb makes the point that, if God chose this universe (this world) with its prevaiing set of physical laws as the stage for the 'arrival of humanity and the incarnation of 'The Second Person of The Trinity', then there must be something unique about both planet earth and humanity (i.e. the imago Dei). Indeed Webb argues that one of the corollaries of Christ's primacy is that humans have the form (and image) precisely because God intended to give a human form to Christ from the beginning. Webb states (unapologetically) that the Old Testament has not only an anthropomorphic view of God but also a 'theomorphic' view of humanity, i.e. that humans take the form they do because God has the form he has—in Christ the Son. Webb makes it clear that sceptics will view his position as anthropomorphism (in the most negative of terms). He understands the reason for the critique well enough but points out that they are mistaken to claim that Christians think of everything from a human perspective and he suggests that "God made the world with mankind in mind, to become friends of the Son and to accompany him in praise forever."

Webb contends that theologians who argue that this world is the only world that God could have created—in their attempt to justify God's relationship with natural evil—run the risk of 'portraying' the world as thoroughly and necessarily evil. That is, if there is no possible world that God could have created that would have been without evil, then the very existence of matter is thoroughly saturated in and inseparable from evil. If evil is built into nature, however, it is God who put it there. Webb's point— that if evil is built into nature, it is God who put it there, clearly rules out the possibility of a third party—or even 'third parties' being responsible for, at least, natural evil. Webb is correct in that God has allowed certain of his creatures the gift of choice and that, consequently, this 'gift' has allowed for the inflicting of an enormous amount of harms. However, this does not mean that God is guilty by default, rather that God has allowed for the kind of creation that is able to express itself. This, surely, is a good outcome rather than a bad outcome. Webb makes a salient point when he says that evil (in the natural world) is real whereas entropy is exactly "what one would expect to find at the level of physical processes". Evil (Webb does not differentiate between natural and moral evil) is, from this perspective, a malevolent factor whereas entropy is, simply, the consequence of certain physical conditions. Webb, however, points out that even though the temptation to equate evolution with evil is understandable. Equating nature with evil runs counter to the Christian tradition, most notably the claim 'exegeted' from Genesis chapter one, that nature is good, which for Webb seems to mean 'moral' rather than 'utilitarian'. My view is that creation does not necessarily have the moral dimension that Webb may wish to assign to it. In this sense nature is amoral. Indeed, Webb reminds us that groups that considered nature evil (Manicheans and Cathars in particular) have always been considered heretical. He maintains that any adequate theological account of evolution has to explain how God (as the source of all that is good) bears no responsibility for evil evident within the evolutionary cycle of life. Webb here uses the term 'evil', but a more appropriate word would be 'harms'—as the results of [natural] entropy need not be considered 'evil' per se. The argument in this book is that neither God's universal laws nor the outcomes of these laws are 'naturally' evil, in and of themselves; they are nothing of the sort. That there are 'harmful outcomes' to these laws is a de facto given; that these outcomes are, most often, horrendous—even maliciously harmful to life's outcomes—is accepted. However, this does not prove that this world is not the best possible world for the purposes of God, neither does it prove that the natural laws themselves are morally deficient. The outcomes of the effects of the natural laws on carbon-based-life may be reprehensible (from our perspective), but that is all that they can be.

It may be acceptable to bring judgement against God with insufficient evidence; to do so is common practice—as C.S. Lewis points out:

> God is guilty—as 'proven'. He (man) is the judge: God is in the dock. He (man) is quite a kindly judge: if God should have a reasonable defence for being the God who 'permits'. The trial may even end in God's acquittal. However, the important thing is that man is on the Bench and God in the Dock.

As has previously been alluded to, Webb's view is that entropy is what one would expect to find at the level of physical processes whereas evil is something other than 'evil'; this demands an explanation. For Webb, the answer to the problem of evil has to be located outside of the evolutionary paradigm rather than within. This is. Indeed, a sentiment concurred with in the argument here— particularly with regard to the 'labelling of nature as evil'. However, the conclusions here are somewhat different from Webb's. His views though are relevant to the argument here, as they helpfully open up a vista that offers some clarity regarding the rebellion of Satan and the angels: Satan's fall is a 'fall from grace' and is not to be confused with a 'fall from heaven to earth'. My argument is that Satan's 'fall from grace' should be considered a 'pre-creation-of-the-physical-universe event'; in other words outside of the space-time-continuum whereas Satan's being cast down to the earth was, probably, not.

We have no detail of 'when' it was that Satan et al. were cast 'down' to the earth, but we can presume that the state of affairs on earth would never be the same again.

Eden was a real place though not 'real' in the sense that we can plot its coordinates on the space-time-continuum that we experience today. If Eden is a real place, and if Satan tries to battle God in nature from some point in the space-time-continuum then there has to be some kind of 'reality' that divides Eden from the rest of the world. The effects of moral deviancy had to cross into Eden in order to disrupt it and, to corrupt its latest arrivals—as Scripture indicates. The 'evil' that Webb refers to is that which can be described as 'moral' rather than 'natural'. This evil comes about as the result of the deviant behaviour of advanced created intelligence: extra-terrestrial and terrestrial alike. The outcomes of this evil, though affecting/infecting certain aspects of the created order, do not bring about major changes to the laws that God had ordained for his creation ordinances—though it may be argued that there was, as a result of this deviancy, a significant change—not least to the effects of the physical laws. The reason for Satan's Fall to come full circle (i.e. the fall of angels to the fall of the creature bearing the imago Dei) is the same reason for creation as a whole, i.e. that God created the world because 'God the Son' had determined to take on the form of a man—and the form God the Father gave to the Son is the same form that God gave to humankind:

> In the beginning was the Word, and the Word was with God is, and the Word was God. He was with God in the beginning. Through him all things were made; without him, nothing was made that has been made. In him was life, and that life was the light of all mankind. The light shines in the darkness, and the darkness has not overcome it…The Word became flesh and made his dwelling among us. We have seen his glory, the glory of the one and only Son, who came from the Father, full of grace and truth. John 1:1-5 & 14 (NIV)

Webb opines that "the world and all that is in it is a gift to the Son from the Father. If something like the human species, with its intelligence, its eyes and who knows what of other parts and features, is inevitable, then biology must have been conditioned from the very beginning to unfold the human pattern" (Webb, 2010) Moreover, Webb's view is that "..This is exactly what the Primacy of Christ leads us to expect. Indeed the Primacy of Christ can be considered the metaphysical precondition made necessary by the phenomenon of evolutionary convergences."

Robert C. Doyle (1999) argues that it is clear from the contents of Genesis chapters 1 to 3, as well as the way Scripture uses these chapters, that the basis for any understanding of the last things is in the understanding of the first things. Doyle's observation is that the beginning of the Bible—the beginning of time, the world, humankind, and humankind's relationship to God and the world—is pregnant with purpose, i.e. the purpose, the end (the eschaton) is implicit in the beginning. Regarding the six days of creation, Doyle proposes that these six days find their significance in the seventh, "…the divine rest on the seventh day indicates the goal of creation." Along with Doyle, we maintain that 'the seventh day' is the goal which shall be maintained,"…despite any rebellious efforts to vitiate it." The argument in this book offers the same reasoning as Doyle's summary, i.e. that God's plan for the creation is purposeful, that it incorporates the alpha and 'the' omega with the telos of creation being finally revealed at the eschaton.

PART3

Regarding Extraterrestrials

"Made a little lower than the Angels…"

That God is 'Triune' is an essential element of the Christian faith—the incarnation of the second person of the Trinity an essential part of the ideas in this book. The notion that Christ[33] should be no more than a prophet or an angel is therefore in error. It is not only in error in terms of unwarranted assumptions from other worldviews, which is particularly the case regarding the teachings of Islam, but it is also in error because it implies a misunderstanding of the person and character of God.

---

[33] Son of Man: Daniel 7:13;John 5:27:Matt. 24:30;Mark 13:24,27; Luke 21:27 Angel of the Lord: Genesis 16:7-14; Judges 5:23, 13:9-22; 2 Kings 19:35; Joshua 5:13-15; Isaiah: 9:6; Zech.1:12. J.

That Christ was a prophet or an angel rather than the second person of the Trinity is not a new idea—though this notion has been rigorously championed—especially since the 19th century, and further explored by others as a part of the 'quest for the historical Jesus' (2000). Or the 'quest for evidence' that would either prove that Christ was a non-historical person, or that Christ was simply 'a man' or [perhaps] an 'angel'—but not 'The Son of God'. (Ehrman, 2014). Louis Goldberg notes that the connection between the angel of the Lord and the pre-incarnate appearance of the Messiah cannot be denied:

> Manoah meets the angel of the Lord and declares that he has seen God. The angel accepts worship from Manoah and his wife as no mere angel and refers to himself as 'Wonderful', the same term applied to the coming deliverer in Isaiah 9:6 (Judges 13:9-22). The functions of the angel of the Lord in the Old Testament prefigure the reconciling ministry of Jesus. In the New Testament, there is no mention of the angel of the Lord; the Messiah himself is this person. (Goldberg, 2009)

Goldberg's conclusion is disputed by others who argue that—while New Testament authors could regard Jesus as "..pre-existent and present with the Israelites in their sacred history (see 1 Corinthians 10:4,9;Jude 5), there is no indication that he was ever identified with the angel of the Lord, not at least until the time of Justin Martyr in the second century." (2014)

Much has been written and continues to be written on the subject. The apostle Paul makes much of the subject—especially with regards to the resurrection of 'Christ', whom Paul assumes, was not an angel and did not become an angel—post-resurrection but rather is THE incarnate Deity—the Word of God, the second person of the Trinity. The apostle's words in 1 Corinthians chapter fifteen clarify Paul's conviction regarding the resurrection of the 'man':

> Now if Christ is proclaimed as raised from the dead, how can some of you say that there is no resurrection of the dead? But if there is no resurrection of the dead, then not even Christ has been raised. And if Christ has not been raised, then our preaching is in vain and your faith is in vain. We are even found to be misrepresenting God, because we testified about God that he raised Christ,…But, in fact, Christ has been raised from the dead, the first fruits of those who have fallen asleep. (1 Corinthians 15:12-14,20)

'*Ecce homo*' (Behold the Man) John 19:5

Michael F. Bird argues that:

> ….among the Church Fathers the strange 'angel of the Lord' in the Old Testament was regarded as an appearance of the pre-incarnate Christ (i.e., a Christophany) a tradition that is as early as Justin Martyr in the mid-second

century…the descriptions of Jesus in Revelation 1:13-16 and 14:14-16 do have angelomorphic qualities as Jesus is described in terms reminiscent of angels…So, is Jesus simply the human manifestation of the 'angel of the Lord'? Did Jesus morph into an angel after his exaltation to heaven? (2014)

Bird most certainly refutes that likelihood though others continue to look for answers that are considered more acceptable. Bird makes the point (in 'of Gods, Angels and Men') that anyone whose presuppositions will not enable them to consider the existence of God let alone the incarnation are not likely to be persuaded otherwise—though an angel may be acceptable for some.[34]Larry Hurtado makes the following apposite comments—referring to the 'remarkable' feature of early Christian devotional practice where Jesus was given the sort of place that was otherwise reserved for God alone:

> Also among the constellation of specific devotional actions involved were songs/hymns concerning Jesus (and sometimes sang to him) that formed a characteristic feature of early Christian worship, the well-known passages commonly thought to be 'Christological hymns' and thus the earliest extant artefacts of this particular practice.

---

[34] Michael F. Bird, Craig A. Evans, Simon J. Gathercole, Charles E. Hill and Chris Tilling add considerable weight to the opposite notion that—Indeed Jesus Christ is the Son of God and not an angel. (2014)

(Hurtado, 2005)

Dr. Michael Heiser notes that:

> …as Christians affirm that God is more than one person
> and that each of these persons is of the same essence—we
> affirm that Jesus is one of these persons. He is God. But in
> another respect, Jesus isn't God—he is not the Father. The
> Father is not The Son, and the Son is not the Father. But
> they are the same essence. (2015)

In his comprehensive work on the identity of the 'Angel of
Yahweh' Heiser puts forward the following arguments, which I
offer here in a condensed form—rather than in their entirety—
though even in this condensed form they are easily identifiable as
of sound argument. Firstly Heiser points out the fact that the
concept of a 'Godhead' in the Old Testament has many facets and
layers. Abraham's spiritual journey includes a divine figure—that
is integral to Israelite Godhead thinking: Heiser refers specifically
to the appearance of the Angel of Yahweh in Genesis 22:1-9. This
passage relates to the appearance of the Angel of Yahweh to
Abraham as, under God's instructions, he proceeded on his journey
to Mount Moriah—where he would offer his one and only son as a
burnt offering. Heiser points out that the angel speaks to Abraham,
but immediately after doing so he commends Abraham for not
withholding Isaac 'from me'! "There is a switch to the first person,
which given that God himself had told Abraham to sacrifice Isaac

(Genesis 22:1-2), seems to require seeing Yahweh as the speaker."
Besides this one example Heiser highlights other examples—
offering the strong possibility that the Angel of Yahweh—is:

Y-H-W-H.

Genesis 26:1-5 marks Yahweh"s first appearance to Isaac: "Isaac
went to…Gerar…and Yahweh appeared to him." In Genesis 26
(vv23-25) Yahweh appears to Isaac again—Isaac receives the same
divine approval—in a series of 'visual encounters with Yahweh. In
Genesis 39: 28-29 we read that Jacob names the place Bethel—
'House of God'—and erects a pillar to commemorate the
conversation he had had with Yahweh (18,19). Genesis 32: 28-29
makes it [reasonably] apparent that 'the man' with whom Jacob
wrestled was a divine being—indeed this mysterious combatant
himself says: 'You have striven with Elohim'—a term that can be
translated either as 'God' or 'a god'. According to Heiser the
narrative, "…nowhere says Jacob's encounter was only a vision.
This Elohim is tangible and corporeal."

*NB.The apparent 'corporeal' nature of the Angel of Yahweh need
not be confused with that of the future incarnation of the Second
Person of the Trinity—as being in the form of mankind—but that it
was, in a real sense a tangible presence—perhaps akin to the
resurrected body of Christ. This is of course speculative but not
beyond the realms of possibility.*

In Exodus 3:12 we read that the Angel of Yahweh appeared

to Moses out of the burning bush. Verse six informs us that, 'Moses hid his face.' Why would Moses have hidden his face from a burning bush—apart from wishing to protect himself from the heat? There was clearly an appearance—a Theophany—the Angel of Yahweh. What does the 'angel' say? Well, according to the text, the 'Lord' speaks in the first person—about His dealings with the people of Israel. In verse 19 we read that—"Moses said to God"—not to a mere angel—but to the Angel of Yahweh who is, most likely, Y-H-W-H. Joshua 5:13-15 and 1 Chronicles 21:16 both explicitly name the Angel with the drawn sword as the Angel of Yahweh. Heiser argues that the connection is unmistakable—on two accounts. 1) Joshua bows to the man—an instinctive reaction to the divine presence. 2) The commander orders Joshua to take off his sandals—because the place on which he stood was holy. There is a lot more to say on this issue, but space will not allow for further comment. The point is that the Christophany referred to as the Angel of the Lord can be identified as the second person of the Trinity—the 'Word' that was to take on the form of man.

Ape-men & Angels

Ape-men

"Adam is a type as real and concrete as his archetype (Jesus Christ),who therefore cannot be reduced to a mere concept or metaphor." (2017)

God, according to current interpretations of evolution, would have (time reference being rhetorical) had no idea what 'Natural Selection' would have thrown up. Humanity may, should Natural Selection have 'dictated' otherwise, have been an entirely different species—even octopuses (*octopodes*); this, of course, is hypothetical but for those who adhere strictly to a naturalistic evolutionary outcome—it may, indeed, have been an 'outcome'. However, it is the case that the argument for the arrival of Homo sapiens would nevertheless obtain. We are meant to be here despite the 'uncertain nature' of the evolutionary process. God surely knows!

According to Genesis 1:26-27 'Mankind' (referring, I suggest, to more than a genetic profile) was made in the image of his creator and given dominion (responsibility for) Creation. For the Apostle Paul, Christ is the image of God—"the firstborn over all creation…" (Colossians 1:15). Note also in 2 Corinthians 4:4 the apostle refers to the image of God which is in Christ. Ergo Christ is the, de facto, image of God. So Christ is the new Adam— or rather, Christ, post resurrection, became the 'renewed Adam'. The point is that if Scripture is referring to a new or renewed 'Adam', we can suppose that there was indeed an original 'Adam'.

Being made in the image of God does not mean that humans somehow are 'god-lookalikes'—neither does it, necessarily, refer to a 'functionality' with, a little more status than paid employees—but rather that mankind has something 'within' that separates him from all other living creatures. Richard Middleton (The Liberating Image: The Imago Dei in Genesis 1) argues that the image referred to in Genesis is of 'vocational calling'—that the 'ascendancy of Homo sapiens' (some three billion years after the creation of the biosphere) allowed the creator God to employ our particular species—particularly in the work of caring for the planet. One might wonder however what benefits there may have been with regards to this particular contract of employment. Moreover, one might further wonder how surprised 'God' may have been to observe the 'arrival' of Homo sapiens if the arrival of our species was out of 'pure chance' rather than out of 'design'.

Regarding the reason for the existence of our 'race' Richard Middleton opines that "Contrary to the popular notion that we are made to worship God, the Bible suggests a more mundane purpose for humans made in God's image, involving the development of culture and care for our earthly environment. But human sin (understood as rebellion and violence) has blocked God's original intent for the flourishing of earthly life." (2014). Middleton's view fits neatly with a theistic evolutionary view of the arrival of 'Homo sapiens'. It establishes some credos for the theistic-materialist view that 'creaturely flourishing' has been the 'sole' purpose for the creation, and shall be so for a redeemed/renewed creation—a creation in which humankind's purpose is functional rather than anything 'extra-terrestrial' i.e.

'sons of the earth and not of the air'. This particular view of mankind's raison d'etre seems to be predicated on a fixation (from creation to eschaton) with an evolutionary interpretation of creation rather than from biblical exegesis alone. This is, indeed, a view that might be seen as 'relevant' to the scientific establishment but that situates the notion of imago Dei nicely within the materialistic paradigm. Could it possibly be the case that this view is fueled by a theistic-evolutionary agenda rather than that of biblical exegesis? Stephen Webb refers to Middleton's position which, according to Webb has "…severed the anthropological implications of the imago from the cosmological…Instead, it should lead us to contemplate the cosmological significance of Jesus Christ, who is "the exact imprint of God's very being." (Hebrews 1:3). The cosmological provides the foundation for the anthropological…

The pre-Fall account of creation describes a world that cannot be compared with this present world—especially with the increase on the demands for the earth's resources and the influence of other forces—one can hardly imagine what may have, otherwise, been the outcome. Even with a hypothetical victory over the deleterious effects of global warming, climate change or the abuse of the earth by latter-day-homo-sapiens, both Scripture and science picture the limits of this present world-order. In a chapter entitled 'Time & Entropy in the Future', Adrian Hough poses, what seems to me to be the obvious question:

If heaven (or a refurbished earth) is free of pain and decay, then what are the consequences for the Second Law of Thermodynamics—and for freedom from the consequences of its effects? (Hough, 2010)

This, Hough suggests, is an important question irrespective of whether a 'are-creation' is seen as 'other-worldly' or as a continuum with the present creation. Should there be any kind of 'future-hope—a 'paradigm shift' from the state of affairs that have been in existence since the creation—or, as is the argument here, since the worsening of that state of affairs—as a consequence the abuse of latter-day-hominids and the fallen extra-terrestrials. Alan P. Ross in (1988) argues that the image of God in Adam cannot signify a physical representation of corporeality, for God is Spirit. The term must therefore figuratively describe human life as a reflection of God's Spiritual nature. Of course, I am not making a case for 'gods' but rather that, according to Scripture and not science, God's purposes for humanity has other possibilities/potentialities. I cannot imagine the scenario that, after billions of years of evolutionary selection, God announces the 'very good': that now there are creatures that can care for the planet. For this purpose, God could have produced automatons—as much as twenty-first-century man seeks to employ the products of artificial intelligence—although these products of man's ingenuity would have, at least, been 'intelligently-designed. I am not suggesting that humanity is not to represent God but that there is so much more to

God's 'design' for humanity. Indeed, I dare say that the 'Functional' idea is bereft of imagination—if nothing else.

C. S. Lewis noted that Christianity does not teach us to desire 'a total release'—as if we were to be emancipated from the physical. Moreover, Lewis considers that entering heaven is to become more human than ever possible on this planet. In one of his 'children's stories Lewis paints a picture of a bleak world in which there is no summer only winter. The 'coming world' may be the world beyond our present experience, but Scripture assures us that life in this, as yet unknown world, is beyond the tainted reach of 'Shadowlands'. It can be further supposed that the paradise of God may somehow co-exist with the known cosmos. In other words, The evolution of the best of all possible worlds (in which, perhaps, entropy has no effects[35]) may have been being created at the same 'time' as this (the best of all possible worlds in which the problem of evil is dealt a fatal blow). The possibility of such a parallel new world order is not, considering the nature and character of the God of Scripture, an unreasonable or implausible assumption.

---

[35] Projecting forward to the actualization of the Grace of God in a 'new world order', R.J. Russell states insightfully that, "in its most simple form it might mean that the New Creation will not include thermodynamics since it contributes to natural evil. In a slightly more complex form it might mean that the New Creation will not include thermodynamics to the extent that it produces natural evils, though it might include it to the extent that it produces natural goods." (Russell 2008).

Moreover, it is not a less reasonable projection than the novel ideas regarding the happenstance of parallel universes. I am of the firm opinion that it is because of the inexhaustible benevolence of God that the 'old order' has been allowed to continue thus far. Moreover, it is because of the gracious mercy of God that every possible opportunity is given for humankind to respond to 'kindness of God' as the apostle Paul refers to in his letter to the Romans. (2:4)

As much as it is possible to offer a theodicy or defence for the goodness and the sovereignty of God, it is quite another thing to satisfy all the challenges proffered against the possibility of, not only the existence of the God of the Judaeo Christian Scriptures, but of this same God's goodness. The argument offered here is as close to an evolutionary theodicy as is possible. There is, however, one area of thought that is in need of more consideration—that of 'Free-Will'. The notion of free-will may be considered a flaw in the argument because, it might be argued that God will have taken a step too far in that any cause and effect from free-will choices would be, ultimately, God's responsibility. In response to this sentiment, I would argue that the free-will expressed in both angelic and human actions were, for the Creator, a price worth paying—and for the creation—a glorious expression of ontological creative genius. The alternative is not a consideration—indeed there would be no need of any notion of defence should free-will be either an illusion or a state of affairs that is beyond the creative ability of an omnipotent God. Let the reader decide which of the two would have produced a better state of affairs: a sterile, mechanistic world void of personality and free-will, in which there existed only the pretence of personality or a world in which God's personality is reflected in the imago Dei—the fallen and the redeemed.

I am in full agreement with the philosopher J.P.Moreland when he states that, "as image-bearers human beings have all the endowments necessary to represent and be representative of God." (2009). The notion of 'being' (ontology), Edgar Andrews notes:

> …means that the image shares something of the being or nature of the divine original, not just his functions (like ruling) and abilities (like language). This does not mean that Adam and Eve were mini-gods: they were, after all, creatures (created things). However, it does mean that they were unequally designed to know and have fellowship with God." (2018)

Theologian Sam Storms suggests that "If both humans and animals are created by God yet the former bears his image and the latter does not, perhaps the image of God consists in some particular feature of a human not found in any [other] animal. In other words, the image is something we possess, some property or properties unequally characteristic of humans." (2018)

So, in what sense did the original humans share the nature of God? Professor Andrews throws significant light into the question when he offers, what I consider to be 'light into the mystery of that image'. Andrews offers what he refers to as a 'four duplex aspect': (1) soul and spirit, (2) language and logic, (3) creativity and competence, (4) law and love. They are named 'duplex' because of the close relationship between each pair. (2018) They are not, as Andrews points out, exhaustive but they are 'explanatory examples'. "More importantly they demonstrate the unique privilege and role assigned to man in creation, and point forward to a future for humanity that the apostle Paul describes in unforgettable terms: "Eye has not seen, nor ear heard, nor have entered the heart of man, the things that God has prepared for those who love him." (1 Corinthians 2:9) That God has planned such a future for those who (on account of their fallen nature) do not love him, constitutes the 'amazing grace' celebrated so eloquently in John Newton's famous hymn—and which lies at the heart of the Christian gospel." (Andrews, 2018)

The 'Breath of Life' mentioned in the second chapter of Genesis (2:7) seems to indicate something more than a physical genesis but rather an indication that there is some kind of imputation into that which is material. Adam resembled God in having a free, rational, Personal Spirit, including a conscience with God's law written upon his heart (Romans 2:14-16);therefore he would rule over nature in a way similar to how God reigns.

The Targums (the ancient Aramaic interpretation of the Hebrew Bible) explain Adam's rational, personal spirit in Genesis 2:7, 'and it (the breath of life) became in man as a spirit that speaks.' Adam, in contrast with the animals, could reason, converse, and fellowship with other human beings. But most important: because Adam resembled God spiritually, he could fellowship with God…The single most important aspect of Adam's creation is that Adam was created in the image of God and his nature bears that image…Whatever position is taken as to the meaning of the image, scholars agree that the essential meaning is understandable—and that is in some way and some degree like God. (2016)

Though this is not the place to develop the argument further, it seems, likely, that much of the thinking surrounding the meaning of 'the image of God' (imago Dei) in mankind is tailored to fit the scientific theory rather than a detailed response to either Scripture of philosophical reasoning—most importantly, Scripture. The view offered here, in contrast to that of Middleton et al., is that: There is indeed so much more to the human species than that of the 'horizontal' or the material—in that there is more to the advent of mankind than being the result of a purely natural process—and an equally material future—even in a 'new heaven' and on a new/refurbished earth. Moreover, surely there is more to the future direction of mankind—both relational and functional—than that of the role of planetary caretaker. Should there be a connection with God's plans and intentions for the creature made in God's image and the rebellion of angels then it is possible that this particular insurrection has to do with God's plans and 'eternal' intentions for the 'treasure in the jars of clay' (2 Corinthians 4:7)—even the sons of Adamah.

> The culmination of God's creative activity in Genesis 1 was the creation of mankind (1:26-28). God formed mankind as imago Dei ("image of God") and thus conferred upon humanity the status of rulers of the earth under the sovereignty of God. God gave mankind a privileged status over the created order. This purpose for humanity's creation is distinct from other Near Eastern creation accounts. In Mesopotamian myth, the gods created humankind merely to do the labor assigned by the deities.(Against The Gods: The Polemical Theology of the Old Testament)

According to Genesis 1:26-27, God confers upon Adam [H]is image and as a result bestows upon Adam dignity, glory, dominion and blessing. This, I suggest has 'glorious' potential rather than servitude—even in the best of environs.

Angels:

It should be noted that there should be no need to assume that the 'time' and location of the creation of the devil and the other angels should be accounted for in the Genesis story of creation. Moreover it is important to maintain the notion of these extra-terrestrial beings as having the will to choose 'wrong' from 'right': to bring about a state of affairs that might not appear to be the preferred will of God but that of the outworking of minds opposed to the good.

There can be no reason why angels could not be endowed with the kind of abilities with which, 'even science', has no present/personal acquaintance. Indeed, even though God the Father is considered to be incorporeal—God, nevertheless, cannot be restricted to any particular 'reality' designated by either science or philosophy—as if God, who is spirit, could not possess, within God's life, such things as personality, will, intellect and 'personal existence'. Angels (both holy and unholy), though usually without form (incorporeal), may, as Scripture makes clear, inhabit the 'physicality' of—what appears to be carbon-based-life-forms. Moreover, as with God, who is Spirit, angels have personal qualities that are far superior to that of humans. These creatures were, according to Scripture, 'privileged beings' with powers that far surpass those of human agents.[36] Hebrews 2:7-9 (also Psalm 8:5) refers to the 'position' of the incarnate 'son of man' who was,

---

[36] These references pertain to the 'position & power' of angels: Psalm 34:7; Psalm 82:1; 1 Chronicles 21:15; Isaiah 37:36, 63:9; Ezekiel chapters 1 & 10. Ezekiel 28. The book of Revelation is replete with examples of such creatures as angels. Genesis 6 also makes mention of their being creatures other than humans 'on earth'; this it can be assumed was a reference to pre-history.

'...for a little while lower than the angels.' [37]

N.T. Wright (1992) refers to the Shema ("Hear, O Israel: YHWH is one...) as the most famous Jewish prayer, "...burned into the consciousness of Judaism in the first century and that it was the battle cry of the nation that believed its God to be the only God, supreme in heaven and on earth..." However, as I shall argue in this section, 'God's so being' in no way precludes the existence of created agents—agents that may be referred to as: 'god's, 'angels' or 'spiritual beings'—the existence of such created beings is, unlike some forms of dualism, not a challenge or denial of the sovereignty of the God of Scripture.

Ulrich Mauser (Mauser, 1991) argued that the supremacy of Israel's God over all other gods—though everywhere asserted—is not a denial of the existence of such 'gods'. Gregory Boyd opines that, while strongly advocating the sovereignty of Yahweh, the Old Testament does include the understanding that, "...Yahweh [must] contend with a sometimes disobedient and incompetent council of spiritual beings (usually called 'gods'), and must, in fact, contend with one particularly malicious god entitled 'the adversary'." (1997) Boyd points out that any reality regarding

---

[37] As Christ was made in the form of a man and had subjected himself to this position (Philippians 2:7-8); he, temporarily, had made himself 'lower than the angels'.

the struggle with other 'gods' is never taken to compromise the supremacy and sovereignty of Yahweh, but rather it is taken to express 'the way in which' Yahweh is supreme and sovereign. Boyd makes clear however that the Israelites did not deny the existence of angelic or spiritual beings but rather that these beings (angelic or spiritual) were referred to as 'gods'; moreover, Boyd also makes clear that these creatures possessed a great deal of independent power. I am in agreement with Boyd—at least here.

Christopher Southgate comments that whatever processes science is able to understand as contributing to the evolution of the complexity, of life: "The richness of ability, the diversity in life', the growth of self-consciousness and the freedom of choice must be presumed to be the gift of God in creation." Southgate is referring here to the creation of life through a material process, i.e. in the earth's biosphere. However, it is, I suggest, the case that such creativity emanates in the mind of God and is not subject to the 'whims' of natural processes; and so it is not at all implausible that this should be the case with extra-terrestrial beings. However, when we refer to angels as created agents of God, we are not in a position to offer any physical (materialistic evolutionary) account of their creation. Genesis 2:1 ("Thus the heavens and the earth were finished and all the hosts of them.") is thought, by some commentators, to include the creation of angels but this may be considered a somewhat tenuous claim, C. John Collins opines that:

The 'heavenly hosts', which some think of (as referring to angels), do not come into the narrative at all. Hence this passage does not answer the question of when the angels were created. The word (tsaba') expresses the idea of a 'serried host' and can, of course, denote the angels as God's army. But it has a wider usage. (2006)

It is possible that angels were in existence before the creation of the biosphere—possibly before the existence of the material universe.

The existence of angelic beings need not be considered a threat to either science or, indeed, to God's sovereignty. Angels are as much a part of God's creative will as anything else God may have created. Richard Swinburne's (1998) view is that "God has no obligation to create". God creates in freedom—to offer the freedom of choice that the creation of conscious/sentient beings allows for—even when this freedom entails an element of risk in terms of the outcomes of any choice. The Sovereignty of the God of Scripture does not entail submission of all of creation to a defined pathway. God is free to choose to create or not to create extraterrestrial and terrestrial beings and any and every biological, or otherwise, expression of his creativity. Creation, through the evolutionary process or any other means, is God's prerogative alone though Scripture suggests that God may delegate that responsibility to lesser beings as James J.Grenshaw (Grenshaw, 2005) points out.

Job 1:6 informs us that 'the sons of God' presented themselves before God and that Satan 'came among them'[38]. We are not told exactly where the place of meeting (Council of God) was located. It is, however, reasonable to assume that it was to be found somewhere outside of the physical universe—at least the 'known cosmos'[39]. Grenshaw states that "Allusions to this heavenly court can be found in texts of various genres, beginning in Genesis and continuing through much of the Bible." Moreover, Grenshaw argues that the peoples of the ancient Near East conceived of the gods—and of these 'gods' as forming a heavenly assembly, "…a kind of divine council…" Psalm 82:1 says " God has taken his place in the divine council; in the midst of the gods he holds judgement." Grenshaw refers to both these texts (Job 1:6 and Psalm 82:1)—particularly regarding the use of the word 'elohim'—as, "…a telling sign that the polytheistic world of the Bible was understood to be more than simply a literary construct." The point here is that the notion of other 'gods' relates to extra-terrestrial-created-agents—agents also described in Scripture as angelic.

---

[38] Robert Sutherland says that, "As a member of the heavenly host and not yet an outside challenger, he seems to have unlimited access to God and the divine council." (Sutherland 2004, 33)

[39] There are numerous scriptures that evidence a 'heavenly council e.g. '…let us go down…' (Genesis 11:7); Isaiah's vision of God (Isaiah 6); 'Ascribe to the Lord O heavenly beings,…' (Psalm 29:1); 'From heaven your stars fought, from their courses they fought against Sisera.' (Judges 5:20); '…Bring down your warriors, O Lord…' (Joel 3:11)

Moreover, as it is clear from Scripture that Satan has 'angelic status' it is most likely the case that the 'sons of God' had a similar status—ergo they may have been angels.

Regarding the existence of the angelic hosts John Lennox (2011) refers to the 'unannounced arrival' of the serpent in Genesis 3—a creature that was clearly opposed to God; a creature that could be described as an 'alien'—not a biological entity but something extra-terrestrial in origin. Unlike biological entities, angels do not appear to have a 'shelf-life'; they seem to be much more durable than normal created entities i.e. entities such as humankind. Moreover, Angels may not, as they are incorporeal/bi-corporeal, be subject to the effects of entropy—the decay, corruption etc. experienced by normal carbon-based-creatures. These 'beings' do not 'rust or decay'—they just exist in another realm in the cosmos or—even in a 'dimension' as yet undetectable by man or machine. Somehow these 'creatures' are given access to this space/time continuum and seem able to do both good and evil—to produce 'good outcomes' and 'harmful outcomes'. The point here is that such creatures are unlike, anything else in all creation, capable of powerful influence within the physical universe—especially here on earth. Ergo, they are formidable adversaries—opposing any good outcomes and encouraging or devising outcomes to the contrary.

Richard Middleton (2005) observes that, although the plurals: 'Let us make man in our image, in our likeness, (Genesis

1:26-28) have been interpreted as a remnant of a polytheistic mythology [referring to the gods of the Canaanite or Mesopotamian pantheon], an adumbration of the Trinity—or at least of a plurality within the Godhead or several other alternatives. A careful intertextual reading of the plurals in Genesis 1:26 suggests that God here addresses the heavenly court or divine council of angels, a reading first suggested in rabbinic commentary on Genesis 1, going back to the 'Targum Pseudo-Jonathan' [40]. Middleton also states that in many biblical texts[41], God's throne room is associated with a heavenly court of angelic beings, who are royal messengers of the cosmic king and who function as God's attendants or counsellors. Moreover, Middleton points out that 'the main action', at this 'time', no longer occurs in the heavens:

> Rather, the dramatic movement of the text is from the heavens (days 1 and 4) to the waters (days 2 and 5) to the earth (days 3 and 6), which is the focus for four of God's eight creative acts. This may explain why on day 6, which foregrounds the earth, there is no explicit vision (or mention) of heavenly beings. Yet their presence is alluded to by the shift from third-person jussives in God's first

---

[40] 'Targum Pseudo-Jonathan rests on a tradition going back to pre-Christian times, though its final form is probably sixth century C,E.' (Middleton 2005,55fn)

[41] Job 1:6;2:1;5:1;15:8;38:7;Psalm 29:1;82:1;89:5-7;97:7;Exodus 15:11;2 Samuel 5:22-25:1 Kings 22:19; Isaiah 6: 2-8;Jeremiah 23:18, 21-22;Ezekiel 1:312-13;10;Daniel 4:17 etc.

seven creative acts to the other cryptic cohortative ('let us make') in the eighth act. (2005)[42]

Could it be that certain members of the Heavenly Council—when disenfranchised—moved their headquarters 'here'?

Middleton's point is that angelic beings[43] are not foreign to the author of Genesis 1 'as is indicated by the occurrence of similar first-person plurals in 3:22 and 11:7 (both of which are usually regarded unproblematic as referring to the heavenly court).' In other words, it can be assumed that there was some kind of plural communication (if not co-operation) in the act of creation's genesis at least. Besides the Spirit of God—some of the 'hosts of heaven' were present on the earth at the very dawn of the birth of life on earth. The witness of certain New Testament passages is that he whom the Church came to confess as the second person of the Trinity was present (Colossians 1:15-20 & Hebrews 1:1-3;10-13).

Simon Gathercole (Gathercole, 2006) refers to what he terms an 'I have come + purpose formula'—as in the pronouncements of Angels. The use of this formula is, Gathercole states, 'not to be understood idiomatically'—as an intrusion into the earthly realm but as a 'coming with prior intent…

---

[42] Isaiah 6:8 is another example of a similar first-person plural—'Whom shall I send, and who will go for us?' (ESV)

[43] Contrary to some objections—objections that Middleton considers implausible. e.g. Westermann, Genesis,1.pp.144-45

138

Gathercole offers a helpful summary:

> Angels announce their advents with the 'I have come' +
> purpose formula. They can do this: a) because they are
> summarising not their whole existence (they visit on
> numerous occasions) but the purpose of a particular visit;
> b) because they have a pre-existence in heaven. Similarly,
> Jesus announces his advent with the 'I have come' +
> purpose formula because he is summarising the purpose of
> his whole earthly life and ministry. As with the angels,
> Jesus is not summarising his whole existence (he will come
> again, with different purposes). However, he does
> summarise his life's work with the 'I have come' + purpose
> formula... (2006)

Peter S. Williams offers, what he describes as, a set of proposed 'explananda' (explicandum):

1) The majority of humanity believes in angels.
2) The majority of philosophers believe in angels.
3) There are various paranormal phenomena that would be coherently and economically explained if demons exist.
4) There are multiple historical and contemporary reports by evidently honest and intelligent eyewitnesses (including psychologists, psychiatrists and clergy) to the reality of Angels and demonic possession (including satanic possession).

5) The Bible teaches that angels and demons (including Gabriel, Michael and Satan) exist (and we have good reason to trust what the Bible teaches).

6) Christian tradition teaches that angels and demons (including Satan) exist.

7) Jesus teaches that angels and demons (including Satan) exist (and we have good reason to trust what Jesus teaches

8) The hypothesis that demons exist provides a partial explanation of how it is that God and evil are compatible realities.

9) Given the existence of God, there is a continuous pattern of hierarchy in creation that seems to come to a unique, aesthetically abrupt and unexpected end, unless angels exist. (Williams, 2002)

It is the case that 'belief in something' (1&2) is not proof of anything other than personal opinion. It is possible that the majority of people may be wrong. For example not everyone would have believed that the earth was flat but, it most likely, would have been, the majority of people (for whatever reason) who held to that particular belief. Indeed there exists still a 'Flat Earth Society. If we take number (2) on Williams list (Williams is a philosopher). The majority of philosophers, we can suppose, are erudite folk—they think things through and come to particular conclusions—though often disagreeing as to what is the 'last word' on the matter; this is particularly true when it comes to 'The

Problem of Evil'—especially the 'Philosophical Problem of Evil'—the Evidential Problem of Evil works better. With (3) it seems to be 'getting warmer': It is most likely the case that 'various paranormal phenomena' can be 'coherently and economically explained if demons exist'.

The late Martin Israel, pathologist and professor at the Royal College of Surgeons, wrote that there is nowadays a tendency to psychologize angels—to identify them exclusively with the archetypes of the collective unconscious. Israel says that, while this may be an accurate enough assessment (of a particular occasion) we ought always to be 'wary of the tendency towards reductionism—ascribing a spiritual phenomenon to nothing but some quirk of the mind.' (1995) Regarding the manifestation of such phenomenon Israel advised that:

> It is much more probable that an angel reveals itself through the archetypical apparatus of the unconscious; in addition, though there may be an incontrovertible physical presence that testifies to its objective reality in our very material world of phenomena.

Israel et al. testify to the reality of such revelations and report extensively of the historicity of such testimonies.

As Williams reports, both Scripture and Christian tradition are replete with evidences/arguments for the existence of such creatures.

It is, therefore, reasonable to suppose that it is the case that Angels exist and that they have a continual influence over both good and bad outcomes. It is also the case that God allows such creatures the freedom to choose either good or bad—to love and serve God or to deny God any allegiance whatsoever.

Given the above detail, we can more than assume that the intelligence, knowledge of angels does not 'emanate' from any primordial source. Moreover, it can be supposed that these creatures are personal beings rather than vague concepts— oppressive systems, power-oriented ideals [mores]. It can be further assumed that they are not restricted to act in the way 'material' objects may be constrained so to act.

'In the Beginning' Angels

In the beginning God created the heavens and the earth.

(Genesis 1:1)

These first few verses from the first book of the Bible provoke both evocation and confusion:

- o What is the 'beginning'?
- o What was there before this 'beginning'?
- o How can the 'beginning' be defined?

In the book entitled 'Genesis Unbound' John Sailhamer (2011) offers a clear perspective as to the sequence of the creation event.

Sailhammer argues that—the 'beginning', as described in verse one of Genesis is a duration of time rather than a particular point in time; his point being that the 'In the beginning' .i.e. 'when' (Hebrew: *reshit*) God created both the heavens and the earth. It is an event that took place in the beginning[44]. The author is referring to 'when'—the English word used by most commentators e.g Robert Alter's 1997 translation (1997). Bruce Waltke (2001) says that, chronologically, this must describe the state of the earth prior to verse one of Genesis 1.

The verses following the first verse offer something other than that. Sailhamer opines that there is "no way to limit this word, it could refer to billions of years, to thousands of years, or to a period as brief as a few months or days." Sailhammer enforces the point that this word (*reshit*) is one of the most crucial words in the entire Genesis creation account:

> In the Bible the term always refers to an extended, yet intermediate duration of time—not a specific moment. It is a block of time which precedes an extended series of time periods. It is 'a time before time.' (Sailhamer, 2011)

---

[44] It is possible that the inspired author was referring to a 'beginning' that was outside of the 'space-time continuum'—but that would be rather speculative (eisegesis rather than exegesis) in terms of the 'comprehension' of such an event. But, it is nevertheless possible.

Considering the fact that there is no evidence in Scripture and no logical reason to suggest that 'Angels' were a part of the creation process i.e. the 'process' that produced the abundance of lifeforms including species such as: Homo Denisova, Homo erectus, Homo neanderthalensis (Neanderthals) and Homo sapiens (Harari, 2014).It may be assumed therefore that Angels were in existence prior to the creation event as described in the first three chapters of Genesis.

Given the existence of the God of the Judeo/Christians Scriptures, the likelihood that Angels pre-existed the advent of the evolution of a 13.7 billion-year-old physical creation is both plausible and coherent. Regarding the question of whether or not angels began when matter began Peter Kreeft suggests that 'angel time' is not the time of the material universe and that angels are no more in physical time than they are in 'physical space'—as matter itself is. Kreeft's argument (with which we concur) is that angels have to enter into this world from without:

> We cannot use the standards of time from this universe—either the revolutions of the 'heavenly' bodies or the constant speed of light to measure how old angels are. Material time is a function of matter, is relative to matter. It does not exist before matter exists. It is between eternity and time.(Kreeft)

There are however contrary opinions regarding creatures such as angels. Christopher Southgate (2008) refers to the work of Andrew Elphinstone who regarded the demonic as something evolving out of the 'necessities of creative process'—not as 'a pre-existent being or beings'. Contrary to Elphinstone's opinion, there is no need whatsoever to suppose that angels were the products of 'the impersonal, plus time plus chance'. Angels were meant to be, and existed prior to the beginnings we read of in the Genesis creation account. Moreover, there can be no reason why an omnipotent God could not have, in a 'reality', other than space/time, created beings that pre-existed the creation of this [our] universe. Indeed, if there were/are in existence other created but non-carbon-based-life-forms, it is reasonable to suppose that they would have been created/existed prior to the creation of the universe.

As angels are, most likely, bi-corporeal creatures and as they were, according to Scripture, 'there' (Job 38:7) at the dawn of creation—they would not have been a part of an evolutionary process—for if angels had they surely could not have 'emerged' until some point in the future rather than the distant, pre-historical, past. Angels do not fit in with a materially driven process—though might fit in with another worldview. However, it would be entirely unreasonable to expect anyone adhering to a materialist (physicalist) view of reality to accept that angels may be created agents of God—though they might be considered the result of an evolutionary process elsewhere in the universe; this though is not the opinion of the author of this book.

> God, when putting Job in his place, asks Job where he was
> when the 'morning stars sang together and all the sons of
> God shouted for Joy?' (Job 38:4-7).

Angels pre-exist the creation of the cosmos and, as I have argued
previously, there no actual record of their creation in Scripture.
There is however an argument for these creatures being created
when 'the heavens were created' (Genesis 1:1)—that the angels
were created during the creation of the heavens (shamayim).
However, this view is highly speculative at the least as the actual
'detail' of their creation is not given in the Genesis text or
anywhere else in Scripture though Scripture does refer to an
angelic 'casting down'.

> Now war arose in heaven, Michael and his angels fighting
> against the dragon. And the dragon and his angels fought
> back, but he was defeated, and there was no longer any
> place for them in heaven. And the great dragon was thrown
> down, that ancient serpent, who is called the devil and
> Satan, the deceiver of the whole world—he was thrown
> down to the earth, and his angels were thrown down with
> him. And I heard a loud voice in heaven, saying, "Now the
> salvation and the power and the kingdom of our God and
> the authority of his Christ have come, for the accuser of our
> brothers and sisters have been thrown down, who accuses

them day and night before our God. (Revelation 12:7-10)

In his commentary on Revelation Dennis Johnson (2001) states that:

> ...the battle that issues in the dragon's expulsion from heaven is not the primeval conflict before Adam's fall when Satan and the other angels who had (we can assume) been created good inexplicably turned against their Creator. Rather, the war in heaven that John sees in symbol was fought on earth, when Jesus suffered and died on a cross outside of Jerusalem...The dragon's banishment from heaven to earth marks the coming of God's kingdom and his Christ's authority. (Revelation 12:10) (Johnson, 2001)

Greg Boyd (1997) refers to 'the warfare worldview' of the Old Testament, in which it affirms the reality of an unseen battle as well as God's ability to vanquish any opposition and to bring about an orderly state of affairs:

> What's more, while many today understand angels to be rather innocuous creatures, mere extensions of God's will, lacking a mind and volition of their own, the Old Testament authors everywhere assume that these 'gods' have a good deal of autonomous power.

Boyd states that appreciating this autonomy is crucial for an understanding of the Old Testament's view of evil[45] —and for an adequate comprehension of how this Old Testament thought developed into what is found in the New Testament. And, it is here that there we find categorical examples of that autonomy:

> For although there may be so-called gods in heaven or on earth—as indeed there are many 'gods' and many 'lords'— yet for us there is one God, the Father, from whom are all things and for whom we exist, and one Lord, Jesus Christ, through whom are all things and through whom we exist.
>
> (1 Corinthians 8:5,6)
>
> In their case the god of this world has blinded the minds of the unbelievers, to keep them from seeing the light of the gospel of the glory of Christ, who is the image of God. (2 Corinthians 4:4)

There are many other examples referring to the influence of (extra) terrestrial' personalities—principalities and powers. One further consideration regarding the existence of angels is that, should angels have been created 'before' the formation of our 'particular' universe—prior to the 'In the beginning God' of Genesis 1:1, we may assume that whatever 'space' they occupy, it is not one that is governed by the physical laws that are associated with the material universe in which carbon-based life 'lives and moves and has its

---

[45] Boyd seems not to specify to which 'evil' he is referring.

being'. It is an altogether different 'world'—a 'wholly other dimension'. It may, indeed, be Heaven. Moreover, when considering the bi-corporeal nature of angels, we need to consider this 'bi-corporeality' as being distinctly different from that of carbon-based life. As I have argued previously, angels were not created through a process of biological evolution and are not most likely subject to the effects of physical laws. However, it may be the case that the 'fallen' number of the 'heavenly hosts' have lost that privilege and shall, at some point in the space-time continuum, suffer the fate of all life-forms that occupy the present cosmos— they shall die.

Angels and Free-Will

Irenaeus held that, in the beginning God formed Adam, not as if God stood in need of man, but that God might have someone on which to confer his benefits. God's conferring of his benefits though does not exclude creatures other than humankind; this could apply to other sentient beings—and it could also apply to non-carbon-based-life-forms such as angels. The question here is whether God's use of angels is purely utilitarian—are they merely automatons—messengers, servants, aids? The argument in this book is that angels were not created for purely utilitarian reasons; moreover, angels are not automatons. Angels are created, among other things, to worship God—something, in which, Scripture implies (e.g. Isaiah 6 Revelation 4), is found complete fulfilment.

Angels are able to benefit from the most worthwhile/worthy of all activities because they are conscious creatures with mental states such as sensation, thought, belief, desire and act of will (active volition power). (Williams, 2002)

Richard Swinburne says that if freedom and responsibility are good things, it is good that there be angels who have it as well as humans. The point is that: If any or all actions performed by the created order (whether angels or humans) were entirely the 'programmed' results of a divine puppet master—this could not possibly be a good state of affairs—not even for God. Swinburne argues that:

> …if it is good that God should give us the ultimate choice over the period of our lives on Earth of being able to fix our characters beyond further change, it would seem to be similarly good that God should give to angels also the ultimate choice of being able to fix their characters. (Swinburne, 1998)

Regarding the likelihood of free-will and the existence of an omnipotent, omniscient, benevolent God, Eleonore Stump (2012) refers to the argument that states that any notion of a human tendency to moral wrongdoing is incomparable with the existence of the God who is omnipotent, omniscient and benevolent. Stump's argument can equally be applied to free-will in angels.

The argument is as follows:

> Humans (also angels) have a propensity to moral wrongdoing.
>
> A propensity to moral wrongdoing is itself an evil.
>
> If there is a perfectly good, omnipotent, omniscient God, he would prevent or eliminate any evil in the world unless he had a morally sufficient reason to allow it.
>
> There is no morally sufficient reason for God to allow the human (angelic) propensity to moral wrongdoing. Therefore, there is no perfectly good, omnipotent, omniscient God.

Stump's conclusion on the matter is that "…to suggest that [allowing] any propensity to moral wrongdoing is itself evil is mistaken." Stump is surely correct. Why should a perfectly good God disallow the sentient creature (man or angel) such potentiality—whether for good or evil? A world in which there were no meaningful actions (actions with consequences) could not be considered the best possible 'outcome' for God's creativity. For such a world, though full of diversity, complexity and beauty, would be a rather 'grey' state of affairs—lacking both meaning and opportunity. A world in which God prevented any 'bad' outcomes by, either intervening before any such morally reprehensible action could issue forth, or by rescuing the victims from their harmful effects, would be a world in which free-will was impossible or a world in which God acted as a kind of 'Superman'. Should the above state of affairs obtain, Free-Will would, de facto, be an illusion—for actions would have no [authentic] consequences—either good or bad.

My argument is that God's allowing his created agents (Angels and Men) free will as opposed to putting constraints on their potentiality is a good thing. There is, from the perspective of this argument, no neutral position: it is good or it is bad. It is the case, obviously, that the freedom to choose allows for both good and bad outcomes. The point here is that Free-Will is an essential factor in 'God's creation objectives'—for without creaturely freedom, i.e. the 'will to choose' (however limited the choice) creation makes no sense; indeed the very idea that God should desire to create such a world undermines the truth of Scripture and the character and person of the God of Scripture.

Regarding the free-will choice of angels, P.S. Williams (2002), quoting an Aristotelian assay, offers the following view:

> Just as there are, good houses and bad houses, so there are good and bad angels. However, while the house has no say in its value, the character of an angel is the character it has freely chosen. That an angel has the freedom to make this choice is a good thing because it is a pre-condition of the value of freely choosing to love God and fulfil its telos.

However, the exercise of angelic free will to reject God is a bad thing, a frustration of the angelic telos that results in the corruption of the intended angelic nature that is called 'demonic';… (2002)

Free Will, Angels and Sovereignty

God's allowing the free will of Angels, as has already been mentioned, raises the question of Sovereignty. How can God retain sovereignty while allowing the potential for what could be described as, unrestrained freedom? Indeed, what [exactly] is meant by the expression, 'The Sovereignty of God?' A.W. Pink's answer is unequivocal. Pink states that:

> We mean the supremacy of God, the kingship of God, the Godhead of God. To say that God is sovereign is to say that God is God. To say that God is sovereign is to declare that He is the Most High…To say that God is sovereign is to declare that He is the Almighty, the Possessor of all power in heaven and earth, so that none can defeat His counsels, thwart His purposes, or resist His will." Arthur W. Pink…

Pink's view allows for the kind of sovereignty that is not 'all controlling' but 'a sovereignty' that depicts all the characteristics mentioned above. However, the term 'resist His will' may not give the best of impressions as if God's desire is to 'control' rather than allow genuine expressions of freedom.

Alvin Plantinga (2011) argues that 'Christian Theism' involves the idea that God governs the world; that what happens does not come about by chance, but by virtue of God's 'providential governance'. In other words, God is sovereign over his creation. This does not, in our opinion, mean that God controls every single event within every single minute of every single hour; or that God pre-ordains the thoughts and actions of men and angels. There are, apparently, numerous outcomes in the world that come about by either the free-will actions of agents or by the 'happenstances' of natural events. It is as David Johnstone makes clear when he refers to the weather as an example of precisely this.

> Consider the weather. The Bible is quite clear that God is in control of the weather (Psalm 42:7; Psalm 135:6-7; Psalm 148:8; Jeremiah 10:13). But we also know that the weather is a natural process. We know about the hydrological cycle and meteorologists are able to predict the weather with some success (the atmosphere being a chaotic system which makes it very hard to predict, but that is beside the point). (2009)

The point here is that the weather being a natural process, does not mean that God is not in control of it or not able to control it—or, in other words 'able to act sovereignly over it'. In his article entitled 'The Necessity of Chance', Paul Ewart (2009) provides good reason why perceived random events do not eradicate the notion of sovereignty, i.e. God's ability to bring about his purposes:

"The necessity of chance is seen to be not just an accidental outcome of the laws of nature but an intentional aspect of God's creating process that preserves both our freedom and his freedom to act."

Theological libraries are replete with books arguing for or against the sovereignty of God. The question is, however: What exactly can we infer from such a belief when contemplating the state of the world we inhabit and, indeed, the very existence of natural evil within an evolutionary paradigm? It could be said that, if God is to be sovereign over all his creation, it must mean that God has access to it all, whether it is the known universe or otherwise. God could not, logically, be sovereign over any entity that is outside of his 'reach'. However, God's sovereignty does not necessitate a strong measure of control on God's part; rather, sovereignty means that God is sufficiently confident in his purposes, immanent or eschatological, for his universe—that the best of possible outcomes will obtain. Indeed this applies to the outcome of the choices of created agents.

Greg Boyd refers to a common objection regarding, what he denotes as 'God's risk-taking'. Boyd says that if God must risk the fate of individuals, it seems that he must also risk his overall goal of acquiring a bride. In other words, it is likely that God's entire plans for world history could ultimately fail. (Boyd, 2001) According to this view, God could lose the fight. Boyd's is a 'possible' conclusion from a reflection on God's desire to be in loving relationship with freely-choosing creatures. However, it is difficult to imagine that the sovereign God of the universe would allow any adversary the final 'victory'. It can, of course, be argued that free-will choices have unpredictable outcomes but it is not implausible to suggest that God cannot bring about the best of possible outcomes for his creation—whether or not humankind is ignorant to how it may be possible that God has foreknowledge of those outcomes.

Regarding the free will choices of humans, Henri Blocher raises concern when he says:

> Either God does not interfere and no longer has control over anything much; or else God contrives to limit the consequences of human choice, and so is not really playing the game and is reducing the drama of freedom to a superficial effect of no importance. (1994)

Blocher has a point—but not a significant one. The problem is in the notion that 'control' and 'sovereignty' are somehow synonymous. Can we not conceive of a God who is so great that he dares to create agents who can, to some extent, make autonomous decisions? It was C.S.Lewis (1996) who stated that what is 'praiseworthy' about God's sovereignty is not that God exercises all the power he has, but rather God does not exercise all the power he could. Ergo: God is not a controlling 'god', but a God who allows 'freedom to choose' yet will, somehow, enable his plans and purposes to obtain.

It may be a present mystery but it is, nevertheless, a possibility that God can so act. Christopher Tiegreen (2006) says that, somehow, God's sovereignty is woven into free will and that free will is woven into God's sovereignty. Tiegreen is referring to humanity, but it can also be applied to the action of angelic 'free agents' who have the capability to bring the utmost good or to unleash the most horrendous evil. It is the case that the free-will choices of agents (angels and men) can bring about satisfactory states of affairs, i.e. states of affairs that may be considered good states of affairs and not bad states of affairs, but it also the case that such choices may bring about bad states of affairs. Nevertheless God's allowing for creatures with free will is, indeed, a good thing. Indeed it is as Richard Swinburne points out:

> We value the spontaneous pursuit of the good, the pursuit of the good which the agent (angels in this case) fully desires to follow. We value the willingly generous action, the naturally honest, spontaneously loving action. But we value even more that the pursuit of the good should result from a free choice of the agent between equally good actions, that is, one resulting from the exercise of (libertarian) free will. It is good for any agent to have such free choice; for that makes him an ultimate source of the way things happen in the Universe. (1998)

Swinburne further argues that it is likely that the actions of angels may well intervene 'in an already created order'.[46] The possibility of such intervention is indeed plausible—though not specifically a part of the argument here in this chapter; the argument here being that Angels possess free will and that this is a good state of affairs as opposed to a bad state of affairs.

Angels with Intent

It is no coincidence that the Gospel of John refers to the 'judgment of the ruler of this world' (John 16:11). It is safe to say that John is not referring to any 'person' other than Satan. Moreover John reports Christ to have said that, in this world, there would be 'tribulation' but that, nevertheless, he (Christ) had overcome the world"—the flesh and the devil[47]. (16:33) Aquinas refers to the fallen state of the devil when he says: "The devil's sin consisted of his having desired his happiness in a disordered way. However, he could have understood the nature of his happiness at the first moment of his creation. Therefore, he could also have willed his happiness in a disordered way at the first moment of his creation. Any efficient cause not acting out of natural necessity can avoid what it causes."

---

[46]I take Swinburne to mean the present order rather than any pre-existing order of creation that may or may not have been carbon based.

[47] Italics are not in the text. See: John 8:44,10:10;1 John 2:15-17,19,4:4; Galatians 5:16-17; 2 Thessalonians 2:4

I take the above to mean that, according to Aquinas, there would have been an alternative pathway.

In his book on Anselm of Canterbury Thomas Williams (2013) refers to Anselm's question regarding freedom of choice:

> If free choice is the power to hold on to what is fitting and expedient, and it is not the power to sin, does it make any sense to say that the first human beings and the rebel angels sinned through free choice?

Williams reports Anselm's reply to this question as being both subtle and plausible: "In order to be able to preserve rectitude of will for its own sake, an agent must be able to perform an action that has its ultimate origin in the agent him—or herself rather than in some external source…Any being that has freedom of choice, therefore, will thereby have the power for self-initiated action." (2013) In 'On the Fall of the Devil' (*De casu diaboli)* R. Williams (2000) reports Anselm as having extended his account of freedom and sin by discussing the first sin of the angels:

> If God had given them only a will for happiness, they would have been necessitated to will whatever they thought would make them happy. Their willing of happiness would have had its ultimate origin in God and not in the angels themselves. So they would not have had the power for self-initiated action, which means that they would not have had free choice. The same thing would have been true, mutatis

mutandis, if God had given them only the will for justice. (Williams, 2000)

As Thomas Williams suggests, Anselm's reply is both subtle and plausible. Free-Will does not necessitate 'rebellion against authority [God] or a predilection to err'—as if either were written in the DNA of the agent, but it does allow for the potentiality of such a state of affairs. According to Scripture, there is an existent state of affairs. Of course, this raises the question of 'holy angels' and their proclivity 'not to sin'. On this matter Anselm offers the following:

> Since God gave them both wills, however, they had the power for self-initiated action. Whether they chose to subject their wills for happiness to the demands of justice or to ignore the demands of justice in the interest of happiness, that choice had its ultimate origin in the angels; it was not received from God. The rebel angels chose to abandon justice in an attempt to gain happiness for themselves, whereas the good angels chose to persevere in justice even if it meant less happiness. God punished the rebel angels by taking away their happiness; he rewarded the good angels by granting them all the happiness they could possibly want. For this reason, the good angels are no longer able to sin. Since there is no further happiness left for them to will, their will for happiness can no longer entice them to overstep the bounds of justice.

Thus Anselm finally explains what it is that perfects free choice so that it becomes unable to sin. (T. Williams)

Rationale for the Angelic Fall

How you are fallen from heaven, O Day Star, son of Dawn! How you are cut down to the ground, you who laid the nations low! You said in your heart, "I will ascend to heaven; above the stars of God; I will set my throne on high; I will sit on the mount of assembly in the far reaches of the north; I will ascend above the heights of the clouds; I will make myself like the Most High." But you are brought down to Sheol, to the far reaches of the pit.

(Isaiah 14:12-15)

Peter Kreeft (1995)refers to Lucifer as, 'the Light-bearer'—the greatest of all creatures, highest angel, Top Guy next to God—and he rebelled and invented evil—many of the angels rebelling with him:

Their war was a real war. It is not symbolic language. It was not a physical war, because angels do not have physical bodies, but it was a real war, a war of wills, of minds, like a war between paralyzed telepaths. The military symbols we use for it are not too strong but too weak….The war was more passionate, intense, and terrifying than any physical war or any physical symbol can convey. (Kreeft)

Fallen Angels have continued not only to oppose God and to denigrate his character but to war against God. The Gospel of John refers to the arch-angel Lucifer (Satan) as a 'murderer' and 'the father of lies' (John 8:44). John G. Stackhouse (1998) points out that Judaism and Christianity teach explicitly that a variety of angels (led by the archangel) conspire against the rule of God— and the 'good' of the world:

> Islam speaks of the jinn, some of whom are evil and serve Satan, or Iblis. As in Judaism and Christianity, these powerful and malignant creatures once were good….Jews and Christians see evil beings as 'fallen angels', or former spiritual servants of God. These angels or demons rebelled against God's sovereignty at some point in, for want of a better term: 'the remote past' and have since been engaged in an unrelenting campaign to frustrate, if not' destroy, God's work of blessing the world. (Stackhouse, 1998)

Given Anselm's (see above) rationale for the fall of angels it would appear that their happiness would have been conterminous with their status; therefore it is likely that their unhappiness would have precipitated their fall from grace. Anselm's reasoning is that "…the rebel angels chose to abandon justice in an attempt to gain happiness for themselves, whereas the good angels chose to persevere 'in justice' even if it meant less happiness." Ergo the happiness of the unholy angels was more important to them than any cause of an omnipotent and benevolent God, such as God's will for humans and for the rest of creation. Regarding the angelic rebellion Peter Vardy (1992) suggests that:

> What The Fall does express, however, is the conviction that God created only good and this good then fell from its perfect state in rebellion against God. Indeed later writers (starting with Origen and later Aquinas) were to see the chief feature of Satan and the Devils as being pride. 'They refused to submit to God; they wished to be autonomous…'(Vardy, p.175)

Although I do not consider the need for 'perfect conditions' for either angels or men, prior to their subsequent fall from grace, I agree with Vardy, that God creates that which is good, and that 'the presence of God' would not be an environment in which rebellion of any sort should take place. Pride would be a good enough reason for a refusal to love and serve God. Regarding the 'catastrophe of the angel rebellion' Greg Boyd (2001) makes the following assertion, "The greater an angel's potential to soar, the greater its potential to fall: *corruptio optimi pessima*." However, contrary to that which Boyd's view implies, the rebellion of the angels is not indicative of some kind of 'Battle of the Titans'; but rather, it is indicative of God's concern to allow authentic freedom to creatures—a freedom that may have allowed for undesired states of affairs.

It is most likely that these creatures were capable of behaving with a freedom that far surpasses that of 'natural man'[48] and that this will have allowed angels the self-determination to contend for autonomy—a drive to achieve absolute self-supremacy and indeed 'self-sufficiency'. Isaiah describes the 'heart' of the matter:

> You said in your heart: 'I will ascend to heaven; above the stars of God. I will sit on the mount of assembly in the far reaches of the north; I will ascend above the heights of the clouds, I will make myself like the Most High"
>
> (Isaiah 14:13–14).

Viktor Frankl's (1988)[49] comparison of 'Freedom' and 'Responsibility' speaks volumes:

> Freedom, however, is not the last word. Freedom is only part of the story and half of the truth. Freedom is but the negative aspect of the whole phenomenon whose positive aspect is responsibleness. In fact, freedom is in danger of degenerating into mere arbitrariness unless it is lived in

---

[48] By 'natural man' I am referring to the state of mind of our species that would have allowed them but one choice in the Garden (Genesis 3)—that of desiring some kind of self-satisfaction, i.e. that they desired the fruit without comprehending the consequences—preferring this option to that of partaking of the tree of life (Genesis 3:24) and the implications thereof.

[49] Dr. Frankl (1905-1997) lost all of his family in the concentration camps of Hitler's Germany but held on to the belief that there was a God in spite of all his observations suggesting the contrary.

terms of responsibleness... (Frankl, 1988)

As has been stated elsewhere, the existence of angelic creatures (including the fallen variety) need not be contentious. Scripture gives abundant significance to their existence. In spite of there being no account of their actual creation in Scripture, angels are described as 'created beings' (Revelation 4:11)—they are not gods. **NB**. The creation of these creatures—including the archangel known as Lucifer (Satan)—does not need to bear any relation to any kind of biologically induced evolutionary processes whatsoever. However, regarding the injurious effects and influences these creatures were to have within the biosphere and elsewhere there would be 'future consequences' for these particular agents as Scripture attests:

> For they deliberately overlook this fact, that the heavens existed long ago, and the earth was formed out of the water and through water by the word of God, and that by means of these the world that then existed was deluged with water and perished. But by the same word the heavens and earth that now exist are stored up for fire, being kept until the day of judgment and destruction of the ungodly...
> However, the day of the Lord will come like a thief, and then the heavens will pass away with a roar, and the heavenly bodies will be burned up and dissolved, and the earth and the works that are done on it will be exposed. Since all these things are thus to be dissolved, what sort of

people ought you to be in lives of holiness and godliness, waiting for and hastening the coming of the day of God, because of which the heavens will be set on fire and dissolved, and the heavenly bodies will melt as they burn! But according to his promise we are waiting for new heavens and a new earth in which righteousness dwells. 2 Peter 3:5-13 (ESV)

These are hidden reefs at your love feasts, as they feast with you without fear, shepherds feeding themselves; waterless clouds, swept along by winds; fruitless trees in late autumn, twice dead, uprooted; wild waves of the sea, casting up the foam of their own shame; wandering stars, for whom the gloom of utter darkness has been reserved forever. It was also about these that Enoch, the seventh from Adam, prophesied, saying "Behold, the Lord comes with ten thousands of his holy ones, to execute judgment on all and to convict all the ungodly of all their deeds of ungodliness that they have committed in such an ungodly way, and of all the harsh things that ungodly sinners have spoken against him." These are grumblers, malcontents, following their own sinful desires; they are loud-mouthed boasters, showing favoritism to gain advantage. Jude 12-16 (ESV)

D.E. Johnson (2001) suggests that the war in heaven that the apostle John sees in symbol was fought when Jesus suffered and died on the cross outside of Jerusalem and cites Revelation 12:7-9. Johnson's opinion regarding the 'actual' time of the above event is interesting and not insignificant. In terms of the space-time outworking of God's plan for the creation, it is, indeed, an interesting possibility and it does resonate with the actual declaration of Christ when he declared: 'It is finished' (*consummatum est*) (John 19:30). These were not the words of one acquiescing to his fate but the words of the victorious Son of God who had defeated the works of Satan and had rescued the creation that groans. The crucifixion was the ultimate sacrifice: The Resurrection of Jesus Christ being the herald of Creation's release from its bondage to decay and corruption; but, for the fallen variety there became 'new'—hitherto unexperienced constraints—constraints that would eventually see their demise—the eclipse of evil and the realization of the eschaton. 'Things, indeed, were to become exponentially worse.

Though Satan's presence in heaven is referred to in Scripture (Job 1:6, 2:1; Revelation 12:7-9), these examples of Satan's presence (whether literal or literary) are 'past-tense' events. It is not necessarily the case, that Satan still occupies the same place of authority to which he was initially appointed—though Satan, along with the other fallen angels continues to exercise/abuse certain of the prerogatives of power that were given by God from the onset of their creation.

As counterintuitive as the existence of such creatures may seem, particularly regarding evolutionary theory, it is the case that the existence of (angelic) extra-terrestrial life is supported by Scripture and may, therefore, form part of a biblically-based theodicy. N.T. Wright (2006) reminds us that when C.S. Lewis wrote the Screw Tape Letters, he referred to the equal and opposite errors into which people could fall when thinking about the devil— they might take the idea of such a being or concept too seriously— imagining "…the satan as a being equal and opposite to God or to Jesus…" or, conversely, they might ridicule the very idea of the existence of such entities.

The Satan, as portrayed in scripture and as experienced and taught about by many spiritual guides, is flatly opposed to God, supremely to God incarnate in the crucified and risen Jesus Christ. The claim made by the satan in Matthew 28:18, that to him has now been given all authority in heaven and earth. (Wright, 2006) **NB**. It needs to be noted that N.T.Wright's view of Satan seems to be that of a none personal being—'the satan' rather than 'Satan'. It seems that this view appropriates well with an evolutionary notion of material events. Indeed, Wright advocates that it is quite wrong to think of 'the satan' as 'personal'—in the same way that God and Christ are personal but rather that, 'the satan is sub-personal'. However, Wright does not suggest that the satan is a 'vague or nebulous force—quite the reverse'.

However, I fail to see the problem and prefer to consider Satan as (very) personal—so personal in fact that this creature is desirous of the elimination of the 'vessel made of clay'(Jeremiah 18:4 & Romans 9:21). Moreover, a 'vague or nebulous' concept could not, conceivably, have 'personal' objectives.

Biospheric Consequences:

The question arises as to how the [continued] rebellion of such creatures can 'possibly' affect the physical realm. How can it possibly manifest itself in a 'materially driven environment?

Though not explicitly addressing the influence of incorporeal/bi-corporeal agents, Marilyn McCord Adams suggests that when evil (unspecified origin) threatens we can take measures by assessing the risk factors "…be it by taking care not to drop matches in dry forests, by boarding up windows against hurricanes, by sending peace-keeping forces…by working long hours in scientific laboratories to discover cures for crippling diseases…" (1999) McCord Adams is not suggesting that the above are inherently evil though they may be considered 'acts of violence' perpetrated by a 'discernible' or otherwise cause & effect. Whatever may be defined as 'a cause' of any such effects aka 'harms', it is the case that these 'harms' have tangible effects on sentient life-forms—whether physical or psychological. Moreover, it is likely that any such 'harms' have been brought about by the influence of seen or unseen 'forces'—natural or otherwise. Ergo, it is reasonable to suppose that these effects may be attributed to incorporeal—or even 'bi-corporeal' intelligence that are of a supernatural rather than a material source. As it may be allowed for God to affect change to the physical order so it may be allowed for extra-terrestrial forces (incorporeal or otherwise) to also affect change; to suggest that such 'august' creatures as fallen angels can have no influence on the physical world would be, furthermore, to deny Scripture as the letter to the church in Ephesus makes clear:

> For we do not wrestle against flesh and blood, but against the rulers, against the authorities, against the cosmic powers over this present darkness, against the spiritual forces of evil in the heavenly (celestial) places. (Ephesians 6:12)

To suggest that fallen angels do not have the ability to bring about: forest fires, hurricanes, war and disease would be to ignore what Scripture affirms—that the immaterial can bring about changes to the 'material'. If this were not so then Scripture would not be replete with examples of how it does exactly that. Moreover, it is the case that the Creator God is able to influence/persuade the creation into being—as well as "…sustaining all things by his powerful word."(Hebrews 1:3)

Referring to Quantum Theory Richard Swinburne makes the point that Quantum theory indicates the most fundamental laws of nature:

…the laws governing the behaviour of very small-scale particles are probabilistic, i.e. indeterministic; but that, in general, small-scale indeterminacies cancel out on the large scale, leading to virtually deterministic behaviour of the medium size objects with which we interact—tables and chairs, trees and persons. (Swinburne, 1998)

It is not that ways have to be found to justify the unseen interaction between the 'material' and the 'immaterial', but that modern advances in theoretical physics have brought to light ideas that had previously been considered most unlikely.

John Hick refers to, "the idea of a fall of angelic beings—preceding and accounting for both the fall of man and the disordered and seemingly dysteleological[50] features of the natural world." (2010) Hick admits that such speculation has its attractions but views it with some disdain—comparing it with that of the 'old Greek pantheon'. Hick adds that the above idea was, in the first century, "… a contemporary Jewish understanding of disease which seems also to have been shared by Jesus himself." (Hick, 2010) Hicks concern here seems to be that such an idea would be a denial of creation's 'natural goodness' or of a materially 'inspired' evolutionary process. In contradistinction to Hick's or similar views, the argument here is that the intrusion of angels into the material world does not deny the possibility of an evolutionary

---

[50] 'Dysteleological' is that existence/being has no final cause—no 'telos'

pathway; neither does such an intrusion militate against the notion of a 'good' creation. However, our understanding of 'good' is not that the creation was ever 'perfectly morally good', so it has to mean something else. Philosopher Stephen T. Davis' view is that "God judged his creation to be very good in that it was a harmonious, beautiful, smoothly working cosmos rather than an ugly, churning chaos over which the Holy Spirit had moved (Genesis. 1:2)." (2001) The Creation was as God intended. Davis, we maintain, is correct in his assessment of the 'very good' state of affairs that prevailed when the words of Genesis 1:31 were pronounced. It 'was' good! However, this being the case did not and does not preclude the strong possibility of there being some, 'not so good' outcomes as the creative process developed, i.e. the subjugation of creation by its creator.

If it were possible for us to examine the outcome of any deviant behaviour within the parameters of the angelic sphere of [creative] influence, we would, most likely, judge that the outcome was less than good—but that was not the case 'at the time' that God adjudged the creation as being: 'Very Good'. R. J. Russell (2008) points out:

> The Second of Thermodynamics provides an example at the level of physics of what is needed if the consequences of sinful acts are to be expressed physically, including dissipation and disruption, as well as the consequences of virtuous acts of beauty and goodness. (2008)

The argument in this book is that the 'potentiality' that Russell aludes to had been allowed for 'prior to' , i.e. 'before' the expansion of space-time—before the genesis of creation—the 'In the beginning God created the heavens and the earth.' (Genesis 1:1) If the Second Law is the necessary component—the one constant that produces the bountiful array of life that emanates through the biological processes as well as producing the entropic consequences that bring about predation, parasitism, plague and even 'natural disasters'—then its inclusion would have been either an intentional act of the Creator of the universe or otherwise. I advocate the former, i.e. that it was both a necessary and intentional act. NB. This does not 'preclude' the notion of God acting kairologically as a response to an event in chronological time by angels or men—in the case of humankind some thirteen plus billion years after the creation of the universe—or in the case of angels before the beginning or at the beginning of the creation. It is not beyond the realms of possibility (even probability) that the state of affairs that prevailed prior to the fall of angels ceased to exist after the fall of angels—that this (very) different state of affairs meant extreme changes that we, may presently, not be able to entertain or to imagine. Whatever might be imagined by the notion of a world' unaffected/uninfected by the intrusion of minds other than God's, we can imagine that it was an entirely different world than the one we presently share with fallen humanity and deviant extra-terrestrials.[51]Indeed, it was 'a garden in Eden in the East' (Genesis 2:8) that God had placed 'the man'. It was the 'garden environment' which, we can assume, was somewhat different. In Genesis 2:17 the author refers not only to the tree of life but also to the 'tree of the knowledge of good and evil'. C. John Collins (2011) refers to the symbolic references (e.g. Proverbs 3:18;11:30; 13:12; 15:4) and suggests that the use of such language warrants us in finding this tree to be some kind of 'sacrament' that (somehow) sustains or confirms someone in his moral condition—this being the reason for God's banishment of the couple from 'the garden'.

The linguistic use of the term 'good and evil' in Scripture is defined as an actual state or potentiality. In other words 'good and evil' had prior linguistic and experiential reality with regards to the actions of created agents. For any such 'actions' to have real effects there needs to be the 'physical' potential, i.e. the potentiality for incorporeal/bi-corporeal agents to bring about less than favourable outcomes within the biosphere: to interfere with the creation.

---

[51] The idea of there being a 'new heaven' and a new or renewed earth, where there is no disease, pain or death, cannot be seriously countenanced unless there were to be changes to the effects of the laws of physics, Indeed, the notion of 'heaven' would be meaningless because disease, pain and death would continue to be the 'natural state of affairs within this particular new heaven—and on this new earth. In order for the promised New Heavens and the New Earth to exist, it has to be otherwise.

Post Fall Subjugation

God's necessary plans and intentions are not to be confused with Paul's words in Romans 8:20-21 where the apostle states that:

> ...the creation was [subjected][52] to futility, not willingly, but because of him who subjected it, in the hope that the creation itself will be set free from its bondage to corruption and obtain the freedom of the glory of the children of God.

In this passage, as elsewhere in Paul's letter to the Christians in Rome, William Hendriksen (1980) Paul is referring to a 'Post Adamic Fall' subjugation and not to any plans or actions taken by the creator before the creation of the physical universe.[53] In terms of the plain reading of the passage, i.e. the cause and the effect of the Adamic Fall, Hendriksen is obviously correct. However, this chronological view of events does not obviate against the possibility of God's retrospective subjugation of the creation. It is the case though, as Leon Morris asserts, Scripture never assigns (either to 'Adam' or 'Satan') the power to bring about such far-reaching change and that there is, therefore, no reason to think of Adam or Satan acting in hope for the future " ...hope is

---

[52] Greek Hupotassŏ meaning to rank under—denoting subjugation. (Vine, 1109)

[53] NB: It was God who subjected the creation—not: angels, demons or mankind. The subjugation that the apostle refers to, moreover, is not related to the creation of the universe but, specifically, to the Adamic Fall as recorded in Genesis 3

characteristic of God, who may indeed be called 'the God of hope' (Romans 15:13) The Adamic fall is not the last word; the last word is with hope." (Morris, 1998). So, when would this subjugation of nature have taken place? As far as the Apostle Paul was concerned, it seems most likely that it would have been after the event in the garden (Genesis 3:15). Here the writer refers explicitly to the condemnation of the 'serpent'. Paul would not have presumed that God had pre-ordained the present (created) biosphere in order to deal with the rebellion of either 'Adam' or 'Fallen Angels'—why should he? The apostle's knowledge, presumably, would have come from his reading of the Old Testament.

John Bimson (2006) refers to the work of Andrew Linzey (2000) who suggests that Paul's use of 'bondage to decay' refers to 'predation and parasitism—all the apparent violence and cruelty inherent in the structures of nature'. Whatever the focus of Paul's words in his letter to the Romans—the de facto (observable) state of affairs was that: the creation was indeed groaning and (will have) continued groaning until the eschaton.

J.Dunn (2003) Suggests that the allusion is clear and that the theme is familiar. Dunn states that the apostle draws the obvious implication from the function of the tree of life in Genesis 2-3, that death of humans, at least, was not a part of the original divine intention in creation. However, despite some ambiguity, Dunn offers what he thinks Paul might be saying:

What Paul seems to be saying is something like this: (1) All humanity shares a common subserviency to sin and death. This is not merely a natural freshness, a created mortality. Sin is bound up with it, a falling short of God's intended best. Death is the outcome of a breakdown within creation. (2) There is a two-sidedness to this state of affairs, involving both sin as an accountable action of individual responsibility…(3)…this state is the consequence of humanity's refusal to acknowledge God, of the creature's attempt to dispense with the creator. When humankind declared its independence from God, it abandoned the only power which can overcome the sin which uses the weakness of the flesh, the only power which can overcome death… (2003)

Dunn's summary offers a reasonable account of the 'life potential' offered to the imago Dei—in contradistinction to mankind's adherence to acquiesce to another's choice—that of Satan. Indeed, Genesis 3:22 informs us that the man had not eaten of the tree of life, 3:24, and that there were cherubim guarding the way to the tree of life so that they could not partake of its fruit. The occupants of the garden had 'eaten' from the tree of the knowledge of good and evil (Genesis 3:6); this was not at all surprising as the quest for knowledge is empowering. It would have been the quest for knowledge, independent of God, where the problem lay (and continues thus)—the quest for power and personal sovereignty.

Perhaps the same quest sought by Satan and the fallen angels.

God had made provision for the sustaining of the life of the first Adam; The Tree of Life had not, previously, been out of bounds. Physical death was, however, the 'order' outside of the garden. Without the direct intervention of the source of life death was the necessary consequence of one of the fundamental laws of physics: the second law of thermodynamics—what William R. Stoeger (2007) describes as "…the underlying physical reason for the transience and fragility of any physically or chemically based system—any material entity…". Death was natural and yet the possibility of eternal (physical) life seemed to be 'on offer', i.e. within the garden.

If eternal (physical) existence was possible, why should God have included such a defining set of rules? There are two reasons that I wish to consider as 'reasons' for God's inclusion of the Second Law within the laws that govern physical reality:

1) That, in order to produce 'conscious physicality' in carbon-based creatures a process of biological evolution (NB. Not that of a process of purely 'Natural Selection') was the best possible way that God choose in order to bring about his ultimate (good) objectives—the production of 'creaturely

value'—ultimately the imago Dei. [54]However, it is not the case that 'Natural Selection' is a necessary path through which the telos of God would have had to proceed—as if God had no other choice. Indeed, if we zoom forward to the resurrection of Christ from the dead, we see the intrusion of a different state of affairs. The Resurrection and the Ascension: These 'earth shattering events' point us to a 'New World Order'—an order in which the Second Law of Thermodynamics has a different outcome. It is the case that, in our present environment, glasses that smash stay in broken pieces; disease brings death; broken hearts stay broken. Of course the advances in modern medicine do so much to alleviate these 'natural outcomes'. But, dead men do not 'naturally' come back to life. The point here is that the notion of adaptation for survival's sake is not necessarily the result of any initial state of affairs—it may well have been different pre-fall, i.e. prior to God's subjugation of the creation. Moreover, 'the nature of things' may have been 'strangely influenced' by the enemies of God. Yet, there is a new world-order promised in which a different set of laws shall prevail.

---

[54] NB If, as Marshall Perry suggests (2015) 'randomness brings us to a dead-end then Classical Darwinian evolution would have been nothing but a 3.8-billion-year string of singularity events: none of them can be further investigated beyond 'The Fittest Survive and everything else dies.

2) To dispose of the 'moral of evil'—the problem that had manifested itself within the physical cosmology—within the present universe—a universe in which carbon-based-life sustains its temporal manifestation. Moreover, it is within the physical/material reality that evil presently pervades but shall not obtain at the eschaton as God will have completely eradicated its potential source as well as its sustenance.

Belief in the sovereignty and integrity of God leads me to the conclusion that God is working his purposes out and that belief in God's benevolence can be sustained. However, the world 'has been', 'is being' and 'will be' subjected to degredation of all kinds until the eschaton. Scripture tells us (Ps. 24:1-2) that this world and all that is in it belongs to God and yet Scripture also states that, 'the whole world lies in the power of the evil one.' (1 Jn. 5:19) And that, '...an enemy has brought corruption to the earth...' (Matt. 13:28). There is, I maintain, no contradiction here as 'ownership' or 'authorship' does not preclude either intrusion or the 'temporal' out-workings of the decisions of 'minds' other than God's. Gregory Boyd (1997) argues that "If the cosmos is not something of a democracy[55], it has to be something of a tyrannical

---

[55] Whilst not sharing Boyd's particular views of the openness of God I appreciate his sentiments here, i.e. that there has to be activity in the creation that is not under the control of a cosmic puppeteer; this applies to the actions (causes and effects) of both humans and angels.

monarchy." I do not hold that the cosmos is anything like a democracy neither do I suppose that 'sovereignty' necessitates tyrannical monarchy—at least not where the God of the Bible is concerned—'gods' are another matter. What is clear from both observation and Scripture is that the earth is not anything like 'heaven' but that it is a place full of all that might be expected if an enemy of God 'wished to' usurp God's authority and to tarnish God's reputation. This 'present' state—as recorded in Scripture and as observed by the discerning eye—is not an example of chaos ruling over sovereignty or any other kind of alleged (dualistic) cosmic conflict. It is not at all what it seems; it is, in spite of what seems to be 'evidence' to the contrary:

> God's future, and this is more than the future time. It is the future of time itself—time past, time present, and time to come. In his future, God comes to his creation and through the power of his righteousness and justice, frees it for his kingdom, and makes it the dwelling place of his glory." (1999)

Eden is central to God's desire/plan; it was in this environment that God so desired to dwell with the creatures made in his image. [56]

---

[56] In his book entitled 'The Unseen Realm' (2015) Michael Heiser maintains that the description of Eden as "…the home of humankind, deflects our attention away from Eden's primary status—God's home on earth—and where the King lives—is where his council meets…"

Considering the pre-existence of Angels it can be concluded that, though created by God, they were not created along with the rest of the creative order within a biological-evolutionary-system. In other words, Angels were created outside of the biosphere in which reside carbon-based life forms in all their multifarious variety. Moreover, as angels are considered to be far more advanced than the most The event that precipitated the rebellion of some of these angelic agents, we maintain, would have been 'known' by God prior to the 'beginnings' of the universe. Ergo, this would have been a major factor regarding God's planned intentions for the material universe—even the existence of certain physical laws that allow for the existence, of what is considered by some transient observers to be 'Natural Evil'. That is an observation in which this particular transient observer sees rather a different picture.

PART 4

GOD IS STILL GOOD

Previously we have looked, in reasonable detail, at the notion of 'goodness'. I have argued that the creation is good in the sense of it being the best possible creation that would enable its creator to bring about a best of possible state of affairs at the eschaton—a pathway to an eschatological ideal. Moreover, I have argued that the creation should not, in spite of it producing harms, be considered anything other than good as Scripture affirms (Genesis 1:31)—a Sovereign God's 'very good' over the creation. Furthermore, I have argued for the validity of a 'Free-Will' defence, i.e. that without a measure of creaturely freedom— particularly that of humankind, the very idea of any alternative to that offering 'creaturely freedom' would make little sense.

Beauty & the Beast

It is a most likely state of affairs that (should the God of the Bible desire to create a world) it would contain: beauty, diversity and a complexity of creatures. This is such a world.

> O Lord, how manifold are your works!
> In wisdom have you made them all;
> the earth is full of your creatures.
>
> (Psalm 104:1)

James L.Grenshaw suggests that the author of Psalm 104 looks beyond the tiny space occupied by humans, "His sweeping survey extends to all creatures and, more importantly, to their creator. Indeed, his sole point of mentioning a variety of animals and their thumb-endowed rival is to laud divine benevolence and wisdom." (2005) Grenshaw adds:"…although the psalmist acknowledges the predatory action of lions during the night, the consequence of this behaviour is construed as a divine gift." In this sense it can be said that, whatever the purpose of the living organism and whatever the 'life-experience' of any such creature, its creation is a good thing—even regarding some of the less positive life-forms that were in existence 'a while' before the arrival of the 'interpreters' of the evolution of biological life.

Regarding the 'Chance & Necessity' of the evolutionary process, John Polkinghorne (1986) says that "… without chance, there would be no change and development, and without necessity, there would be no preservation and selection." In his later work entitled 'The God of Hope and End of the World (2002) Polkinghorne states that:

> …through the intricate unfolding of physical processes initial simplicity has generated immense complexity… Theologically one can understand this complexity as the result of creation's having been endowed by its creator with a profound potentiality which has been allowed to explore and realise as it makes itself.

Polkinghorne's position is one that envisages an evolutionary-creation scenario in which God does not 'control' all of creation (as would a 'tyrannical puppeteer') but rather one of a creator whose, "…nature of love is patient and subtle, content to achieve the divine purposes in an open and developing way, in which the creatures themselves collaborate." Whatever one may conclude from the above views of the actual level of God's interaction with the physical world; it is this world that allows for such diversity and complexity. It is, however, 'good' for God to have created such potentiality—such complexity, diversity and beauty. One does wonder though about the 'prohibition' that some theists (in order not to be out of step with 'the science') impose on the Creator –even an 'exclusion zone'. It seems as if our present understanding of how the biosphere functions disallows for any notion of interference from The Creator—echoes of:

'We cannot allow that divine foot in the door.' (Richard Lewontin)

David Wilkinson (2009) argues that we need to take seriously the notion that the heavens declare the glory of God (Psalm 19:1), and that, "God may choose to reveal himself through the natural world, the book of his works as well as through the book of his word." This is exactly what the apostle Paul refers to in his letter to the Romans (1:20) where he refers to God's eternal power, invisible qualities and divine nature—'having' (through the creation) been clearly seen…" In referring to the cosmic picture of Christ, Astrophysicist and theologian, Wilkinson states that:

> …this cosmic picture of Jesus suggests that God is the sustainer of order in creation. Paul in Colossians 1:17 reminds us that Christ is before all things, but also that 'in him, all things hold together'. The apostle's picture is a very different one from that of a deistic Creator who lights the blue touch paper of the Big Bang and then goes off to have a cup of tea. The verb is in the perfect indicating everything held together in him and continues to do so. (Wilkinson, 2009)

The heavens, indeed, declare the glory of God. Scripture enunciates the unseen glory that is being revealed in the creation— that God both creates and sustains; that there is an overall 'goodness' about the Creation—that the absolute goodness of the creation will be finally revealed at the eschaton.[57]

In referring to the progress, complexity and diversity of life the paleontologist and evolutionary biologist, Simon Conway Morris (2003) opines that "…when within the animals we see the emergence of larger and more complex brains, sophisticated vocalisations, echolocation, electrical perception, advanced social systems including eusociality, viviparity, warm-bloodedness, and agriculture—all of which are convergent—then to me that sounds like progress." Conway Morris' description paints a picture of an abundantly creative process that may be described as good. Ergo, it is good that God should have so done. Moreover, it is most unlikely that such an abundant array of life could have been produced by any other means than which God designated, or, indeed, by any other deity—'tyrannical puppeteer' or otherwise. Process theologian John Haught (2010) says that "…the fact that natural selection produces design, diversity, and what Darwin calls the 'descent of man' does not exclude the possibility that the evolutionary drama carries a hidden meaning and that it is directional in a very profound sense because it bears invisibly within it the cooperative influence of a liberating and promising God." Haught's 'couched' reference to there being—at least—the possibility of a 'blueprint' within a naturally selective process is

---

typical of those who identify as theists (of varying shades) but who do not want to be associated in any way with creationist notions. However, I am pleased to affirm that the creation is, indeed about 'the liberating promises of God'. It is the 'liberation and promises' of God that are germane to the argument here for evolution per se cannot offer either promise or liberation; however, the God of the Christian Bible is able to bring about such profound 'coincidences'. The creator God whose character is such that He cares passionately for all that He has created and promises to liberate.

<u>God promises to liberate creation from its 'groaning,'</u> i.e. the creation that God Himself has brought under subjugation. This subjugation though should not be thought of in a utilitarian way— as if the ephemeral appearance of the `billions of creatures over the course of time were simply a means to a 'convergent' end—that [all] of creation has no true value to its creator. Moreover, the giving of himself in creation underlies God's character—especially his 'Triunity'. Douglas Meeks (2006) has said that the doctrine of the [social] Trinity claims that God's 'owning' is not grounded in self-possession but rather in self-giving: "It is the character of God to give God's self to us and to give us all things with God's self (Romans 8:32). God owns by giving…It is God's self-giving which, is the font of human livelihood in community." (Meeks, 2006) God creates in order to show both his Glory and His Benevolence, i.e. God sharing His life with carbon-based life-

forms. Is that not a 'good thing?' God would have, surely 'rejoiced' in the results of the creative process that, profusely, established life in all its diversity throughout the earth, seas and skies. It was this amazing array of life that inhabited this 'bright-blue-sphere'—eons before the arrival of mankind. Before the shadow of man's presence on earth, there existed a creation that may not have been 'read by its critiques' as being 'red in tooth and claw'. Indeed, there existed no carbon-based life-form that could have set itself up as judge and jury. Creation, as the author of Genesis (1:31) announces, was and is very good.

Prior to the advent of modern man there would not have been any 'palpable' sense of moral 'indignation' proffered against the author of creation; the creation would have been amoral in its character yet it would nevertheless have been a 'good' creation as it would have been the creation of a benevolent deity. But this [Creation] alone, without either the emergence of the creatures that are allowed the freedom of accusation—or the appearance of the accuser [Satan] who neither loved God or acknowledged God's right to rule, could never have been a completed work. For it has been the telos of God to create such a species as mankind and for God, the Son, to 'put on frail flesh and die'—so that the creation could be released from its bondage to decay, and Christ's victory over [moral] evil could be finally won:

> ...the ancient patristic understanding of theosis—the view that God's purposes in creating included his desire, from

the beginning for the 'divinization' of humankind through the hominization of Christ…And the divine love has always willed that the journey of creation and pilgrimage of humanity should end in our final adoption as coheirs of God's kingdom and "partakers of the divine nature". (Osborn, 2014)

This 'final adoption' as co-heirs of God's Kingdom shall be realised at the Eschaton. This realization shall bring with it another world order—either here on earth or in a new cosmological world-order. Moreover, this is the 'release' that occurs at the Eschaton—when there shall be a new-world-order—an order rather different than this present state of affairs in which the effects of certain physical laws dictate negative outcomes. As I have argued previously, this new-world-order has to be 'other than this present system—governed by physical laws that prevent it from being anything like the promised 'new heavens and new earth. The implication is clear: When the eschaton occurs there shall be another order—either here or elsewhere. I suspect an 'elsewhere' as, I cannot see a justifiable reason, given God's benevolence—alongside God's omnipotence, for an 'earthly refurbishment'—which would be temporary at best.

Prior to offering his own compound evolutionary defence for the goodness of God—in the face of 'The Groaning of Creation', Christopher Southgate reconsiders the implications of a 'very good creation'—concluding that creation is good in its proclivity to give rise to what Southgate refers to as, "…great values of beauty, diversity, complexity, and ingenuity of evolutionary strategy…Moreover, Creation is also good because it is God's Creation (Ps.24:1). There are several points to be taken from Southgate's view of the creation: Creation, in the light of an evolutionary process, is undeniably prolific—its diversity, complexity and beauty beyond the realms of coincidence or 'coincidental' convergence—one might suggest.

o   Creation declares the glory of God, and whatever declares the glory of God is a 'good thing'.
o   That God's concern for the creation is personal.
o   That the Triune God (Father, Son, Holy Spirit) continually sustains the present creation.
o   That, in Christ and for Christ, God 'is preparing' a created order (new heavens & new earth)…So that God's ultimate GOOD purposes shall obtain.

As amazingly beautiful and prolific the biosphere it may be, it is nevertheless a 'vale of tears' (*vallis lacrimarum*) for much of its sentient sojourners. The words of Revelation 21:5 ring loudly in our longing for 'home': "Behold I shall make all things new…" This earth we inhabit was never meant to be 'Heaven'—there never was a perfect environment in which there were no danger of harms—there was but a 'garden in Eden—in the East **NB**

If a replenished planet earth is to be the abode in which the redeemed shall dell, there would have to be some, more than significant, changes to the physical laws— the laws that necessitate certain effects on carbon-based life-forms. Laws, however, that allowed for the incarnation of God the Son—for the redemption of a creation in the pangs of childbirth.

An evolutionary 'devil' in the detail

In a chapter entitled 'Evolutionary explanation' Professor Ian Hutchinson (2011) refers to the dangers of a hospital environment. Hutchinson comments that one reason hospitals are such dangerous places is that, "…the environmental pressures on the bacteria there (in hospitals) are such that they rapidly evolve resistance to the various anti-bacterial agents that hospitals use."

Within the biospheric 'framework' there are a quite remarkable amount of life-forms, some of which might be considered unnecessary intruders, or the kinds of creation that God would 'surely not have conjured-up' because they seem to prove a contradiction in terms when one maintains a particular understanding of what a 'good' creation would look like. Bacterial life-forms are, as Hutchinson infers, endemic—not only in hospitals but in the whole of the biosphere. They are essential to the whole of the history of the biosphere. Biochemistry Professor and Intelligent Design proponent Michael Behe (2007) refers to statistics offered by workers at the University of Georgia who estimated that about a billion billion trillion (thereabouts) bacterial cells are formed on the earth each and every year. Behe adds that:

If that number has been the same over the entire several-billion-year history of the world, then throughout the course of history there would have been slightly fewer than 1040 cells, a bit less than we'd expect to need to get a double CCC (i.e. a mutation cluster: 'chloroquine-complexity clusters'): The conclusion, then, is that the odds are slightly against even one double CCC showing up by Darwinian process in the entire course of the life on earth…So if we do find features of life that would have required a double CCC or more, then we can infer that they likely did not arise by a (purely material) Darwinian process.

Biochemist, Dennis Alexander refers to the necessary effects of biological evolution on its products—advocating that biology is a package deal and that the values only come with the disvalues. However, Alexander goes on to say that the positive side of this is that we are living in an incredibly dynamic world in which there is what he refers to as 'a huge amount of daily coming and going—the dead of all kinds are constantly making room for the living; all of life is Interdependent' . Alexander holds that the God of all creation is also the great naturalist who enjoys all the richness and diversity of the natural world that he has brought into being—including its 'impressive carnivores' . John Polkinghorne underlines the fact that this current universe is a creation endowed with the physical properties that have empowered it to 'make itself' over the course of its evolutionary history: "A world of this kind by its necessary nature must be a world of transience in which death is the cost of new life. In theological terms, this world is a creation that is sustained by its Creator, and which has been endowed with a divinely purposed fruitfulness,…" Of course, it is the case that a 'divinely purposed fruitfulness' offers no guarantee of a 'just so world' in which there is no cost to the created order—unless it can be argued that the God of the Bible had no choice but to initiate such a 'chamber of horrors—that this world is, not only the 'best possible world' but the 'only possible world in which God could bring about his 'GOOD' purposes. This world may be 'endowed by collaboration and fruitfulness', but it is also a 'vale of tears' in which, metaphorically speaking, 'all hell breaks loose'. Such a world as this most definitely necessitates suffering, but whether or not its proclivity to produce the 'short successes' of life—the inevitability of pain and extinction may be considered wasteful—may not be comprehensively addressed from mankind's current knowledge or current perspective. God is, as John Polkinghorne suggests:'…the one who holds creation in being and interacts in hidden ways with its history. It is though 'the hiddeness' that mankind finds so difficult to comprehend. What may be observed 'today', is not the whole story. Polkinghorne refers to the "two halves of God's great creative/redemptive act…" —the second half being that through which God shall bring about both vindication and justification for the [Created] state of affairs. The 'present' half (the old creation) may be seen to explore and realise its potentiality at "some metaphysical distance from its Creator" while the second half—the new redeemed creation—is brought into freedom through its intimate relationship with the 'life of God'—in and through the work of Christ. The problem with this is of course: How to balance the evidence for a 'greater-good' with the opposite.

In philosophy much is spoken of regarding the existence of a 'Best Possible World'—that in order to offer a defence for the existence of evil in the world this world is to be defined as 'the best possible world'. "Supreme wisdom—united to a goodness that is no less infinite cannot but have chosen the best…" (Leibniz) In other words, the God of the Bible would have had to create the best possible world. Ergo, this world is the best [of] possible states of affairs. But is that the case? Moreover, need it be so? Christopher Southgate says that he fully accepts that we can never be sure that this was God's only way to give rise to creatures such as stem from the 3.8-billion-year-long evolution of the Earth's biosphere but he does suggest that, "…given what we know about creatures, especially what we know about the role of evolution, in refining their characteristics, and the sheer length of time the process has required to give rise to sophisticated sentience, it is eminently plausible and coherent to conclude that this was the only way open to God." It seems to me that Southgate is sacrificing the omnipotence of God in order to retain God's benevolence—or indeed to avoid conflict with the present 'priestly' paradigm of evolutionary theory or, indeed, the latest 'synthesis'. However, there are several things that can be said in answer to this. Firstly, in the light of our comprehension of the evolutionary process so far, we can ascertain certain fundamentals of the evolutionary process—fundamentals that Southgate mentions: 1. The role of 'evolution' in the refining of creatures' characteristics. 2. The amount of time taken. There are also several things we can say about Southgate's assumptions:

> That, given the nature of God's omnipotence we can presume that time and procedure had nothing to do with God's ability but all to do with God's planned intentions— intentions to produce intelligent carbon-based-life on this planet. i.e. That there always has been—for want of a better word—a 'blueprint' for the process. It was never left to mere 'chance'—for if it had been, we need not look further for omnipotence; though benevolence we might find— though it would be a poor substitute—and would hardly give us cause for rejoicing. God's role in this procedure would have been one of watching 'helplessly/haplessly' by as a mother watches her fledgeling bird being devoured by its predator. That given God's omnipotence we can further assume there was no 'better' way for God to bring about/to actualize particular outcomes.

Critics demand to know why it is that, in spite of God's 'alleged' attributes, this world appears to fall far short of being the 'best possible world'.

Michael Murray (2008) considers two sorts of criticism: 1) that the natural laws could have been better and 2) that there could have been more 'evil-preventing interventions'. Murray's suggestion is that, to show that such a world is possible the critic would need to describe a nomically regular world which (a) contains goodness of the sorts (either the same sorts or equivalent or better sorts) and amounts found in the actual world and which (b) contains substantially less natural evil than the actual world. Murray's conclusion is that the task seems hopeless—that it would be necessary to identify a reasonably complete list of the goods that this actual world contains in order to offer a 'best possible world' potentiality. He suggests that it would be hard to know whether or not the acquisition of such a comprehensive list was at all possible: "Not only must the critic confront the fact that describing such an alternative world is seemingly beyond our capacities, she must also confront the claims of numerous scientists that there are many respects in which the physical parameters governing our world could not, after all, be significantly different from what they are in fact." Murray's points are crucial to the question of whether or not God could have presented a better option. Murray, I believe, is most likely correct: As from our present understanding of the physical world—we cannot know whether or not there could have been a better option; this world being de facto the world we inhabit and of which we have reasonably comprehensive knowledge. As I have suggested elsewhere: It is not beyond the realms of possibility/probability that a different manifestation of the physical laws existed prior to the Angelic Fall— i.e. physical laws that might have preceded the 'known laws of physics—the Nomic Regularity' that Murray makes much of in his aforementioned book. Most importantly, it is because of the character of the God of Scripture, that we can assume that this world is the best of possible worlds. Liebniz indeed argues that it is in this sense that this world is the best possible world, as we know of no other, and assume that God would not have created this world without it being an absolute necessary state of affairs; this is, as is suggested above, an assumption rather than an argument—it is though a reasonable assumption. Alvin Plantinga (1974) quite rightfully, points out that Leibniz' view (his lapse)—that an omnipotent God could have created/actualized just any world God pleased is false; this is taken to mean, according to this reasoning, that God could not have created a world in which there was neither natural or moral evil. This world, as is 'painfully obvious', contains states of affairs that are considered to be rather bad states of affairs—states of affairs that, it can be concluded are brought about by both 'natural' and 'moral' evil. However, this world is, nevertheless, the best possible world, in that it is in this kind of environment in which the freedom of the action of carbon-based-life and (even) none-carbon-based-life expresses itself—and in which the actions of both men and angels have both good and bad outcomes. Moreover, it is this world that God has created so that both freedom and justice may obtain i.e. the freedom of the 'will to do'—of Angels and of Men. And, moreover, the freedom of an omnipotent and benevolent

God—so that God may bring about a just state of affairs in accordance with God's perfect governance i.e. God's plans and purposes to 'tabernacle' with the Jewel of his creation—the imago Dei.

If God were to create a world in which there existed only good outcomes, it would not be a world in which freedom could, in real terms, express itself because neither action or an outcome would have moral veracity as both would be neutral—neither good or bad. I hasten to add here that—the question of 'free-will' is crucial both to the goodness of God and to God's reason for Creation. Moreover, it does not bring into question the 'Sovereignty of God'.It is in this, the best of possible worlds, that the first part of Polkinghorne's (2002) two-stage act of God's creation plan can be actualised: The first-stage being the present scenario—subject to the effects of entropy, and the second-stage following on from the eschaton—'new heavens and earth'. Polkinghorne's scenario though does not offer a defence for God's use of the evolutionary process but rather brings a focus on a future (eschatological) finality where all may be considered 'well'.

Listed in what he refers to as the core of his approach, Christopher Southgate states that there is a strong likelihood that, "…an evolving creation was the only way in which God could give rise to the sort of beauty, diversity, sentience, and sophistication of creatures that the biosphere now contains." Southgate qualifies this by stating that this is, indeed, an '(unprovable) assumption'.

Southgate's assumption is, indeed, unprovable. Furthermore it is, from a Christian perspective, an unnecessary assumption as there are better options.

Given that the overwhelming consensus of both science and philosophy is that evolution is the most likely means through which all carbon-based-life came into existence, it is extremely likely that—from these perspectives—Southgate is correct in his assessment. However, it is not 'just' that an evolutionary 'creative' process has, seemingly, been the only way through which such a rich tapestry of life could have developed. It is also the case that (*because of the biospheric potentiality*) the evolution of creatures with the potential for higher-order-thought (the emergence of the creature with the physiological potential for becoming the creature that reflects God's image) has, according to this view, been possible. From this perspective, it may be said that it (evolution) has been the means through which God has brought about the best possible outcomes—for His [good] purposes. It is assumed, therefore, that God does bring about his created objectives—even through what appears (presently) to be random processes. Dennis Alexander (2008) poses the question of how a good God could choose to bring about all of the biological diversity, including us— by such a long and wasteful process—a process that involves so much death and suffering? As has been mentioned elsewhere Alexander comments,regarding the positive side of nature's cycle of: predation, parasitism, plague etc., that we are living in an incredibly dynamic world in which there is what Alexander refers to as 'a huge amount of daily coming and going—the dead of all kinds are constantly making room for the living; all of life is Interdependent'. Alexander holds that the God of all creation is also the great naturalist who enjoys all the richness and diversity of the natural world that he has brought into being—including its 'impressive carnivores'. However, Alexander's picture of the 'great naturalist' enjoying the sight of one section of his handiwork tearing apart the other is not one that speaks of benevolence, rather of a sort of divine utilitarianism. NB. If the process is simply a means to an end, what end might that be?

In terms of the 'end-game' being a 'redeemed' version of our amazing 'planet earth', it is difficult to imagine this 'new order as an environment wherein the physical laws don't continue to have the same deleterious effects—especially when reconciling the biospheric marvel that has taken millions of years to evolve—with that of an earthly paradise (or even a garden to work in) that will (with God's intervention) evolve out of the present (post-industrial revolution) model—into the paradise in which there shall be 'no more crying and no more dying'. How would it be possible to reconcile this with an 'earthly' heaven? Then there is the possibility of the occasional collision of large meteorites and subsequent ice-ages—or, more likely the opposite. Of course, God may well bring about a different state of affairs wherein God protects his new creation from all the other potentially, i.e. the big crunch', heat-death or 'freeze out'. This, I suggest, has to be a better option for an Omniscient, Omnipotent, and Benevolent Deity.

As one of the theological problems with which this book wrestles is that of suffering within evolution, it is my intention not to 'muddy the waters' with 'fine sounding arguments' that have no substance—at least no substance when it comes to the defence of Christian belief and practice. Christopher Southgate notes that the problem of suffering (aka 'natural evil') within a 'theistic evolutionary paradigm' has several aspects one of which is that if God created this system, which is full of suffering, then the goodness of God seems to be in question. Another is the question raised previously in respect to Alexander's ideas:

Did God use suffering within evolution as a means to 'the divine ends'? It is the opinion of the author that this is not the case.

Alister McGrath (2011) brings the issue into focus by noting that Darwin's model of evolution envisages the emergence of the animal kingdom as taking place over a vastly extended period of time, involving suffering and apparent wastage that go far beyond the concerns of traditional theodicy. McGrath notes that Darwinism intensifies existing concerns with the problem of suffering. With evolution comes suffering and death—they are a part of the same package. If God is able to create all the necessary material and has the wherewithal to envisage and bring into being the best possible world—and yet has, seemingly, failed to accomplish his objectives without huge concomitant suffering, then there are bona fide reasons for seeking answers as to why this seems not to be the case. But, is it the case at all? What if there is far more going on than God's desire to create 'a best of possible worlds'? As has been stated previously, the prevailing view, of both science and philosophy, is that a system of biological evolutionary development is the only way through which all the 'values' of all the creatures that have ever existed could obtain. Ergo: predation, pain, parasitism, plague and (obviously) death, are all instrumental in the processes that produce the values to which Christopher Southgate refers, i.e. That a Universe (world) in which complexity emerges in a process governed by thermodynamic necessity and (Darwinian) Natural Selection—is the only sort of universe that could give rise to the beauty, complexity, and diversity of creatures the Earth has produced.

If Southgate is correct—and if the New Heavens and New Earth (Isaiah 65:17,66:22; 2 Peter 3:13 & Revelation 21:1) are 'of the same stuff'—and under the 'jurisdiction' of the same physical laws, then there would be no reason to expect anything much different than that of a reconditioned planet earth. It is not that this world is not the best of possible worlds. But, it is the case that the notion of 'a best possible world' has nothing whatsoever to do with the idea that God could not have achieved his creation objective without such a protracted system of biological evolution. On the contrary, this is not the best of possible worlds in which the God of the Bible would bring into being: New Heavens and a New Earth'—as if at the end of billions of years of evolution there would appear a world in which there would be no: crying pain or death. But, this is the best of possible worlds in which justice would ultimately obtain—a world in which Christ would offer the greatest sacrifice and a world in which God would bring to justice—both men and angels. For the wages of sin is [indeed] death, but the gift of God is eternal life.' (Romans 6:23) It is for this reason alone that this present world is the best possible world. To suggest that God is limited to the present model will have 'missed the point'. How would predation, parasitism, plague not be a part of a world in which the same physical laws prevailed?

There is more to the narrative than the (theistic) evolutionary just-so-story would have us believe? I can fully accept that it is not possible to know whether or not the evolution of the earth's biosphere was God's only way to bring about God's planned intentions—even though the standard response from theistic evolutionists would be that it was, most likely, God's only option. That God might have had the 'one option' does not preclude the likelihood of God's omnipotence i.e. that God, by divine fiat could not have commanded the whole of nature to appear at once or even over the course of a few thousand years—or even over a twenty-four-hour-period. Of course, should either of these options have been actual-events then creation's rich tapestry of life would never have existed or would not have reached its 'zenith'. However, it might be the case that God is an 'underachiever'—not at all 'all powerful' and 'all knowing'. If God were to be considered so inept a deity, God could hardly be described as omnipotent—this though would depend on the end (telos) of God's purposes rather than the beginning.

In contradistinction to arguments given by some Theistic Evolutionists, my argument is that God's desire was to bring about a state of affairs that allowed for the 'arrival' of carbon-based life forms—in particular the imago Dei—with independent characteristics allowing for the 'arrival' of free-will—the interaction of 'mind' and body. Some may object, and talk of 'fairies' or even 'magic'—'fairy stories and magic' indeed.

With regards to the notion of free-will (aka the extraordinary consciousness/ability that the human race has over and above that of other creatures) he atheist philosopher Daniel Dennett wrote the following regarding its alleged evolution:

> Since I am conscious and you are conscious, we must have conscious selves…How can this be? To see how such an extraordinary composition job could be accomplished we need to look at the history of the design processes that did all the work—the evolution of human consciousness. We also need to see how these souls made of cellular robots actually do endow us with the important powers and

resultant obligations that traditional material souls were supposed to endow us with (by unspecified magic)." (2003)

Magic' apart, though it has to be said that 'naturally' driven evolutionary coincidences provoke thoughts of magic—of 'magicians' and of 'just so stories'. It is the question of the notion of the evolution of consciousness—of its 'evolving' freedoms from a source other than Natural Selection that, seemingly, divides opinion in evolutionary interpretation. Clearly, from a materialist perspective, any idea that the 'none material' can interact/interfere with the 'material', the 'physical'—the biological is a non-sequitur. However, from a theistic perspective, there need be no such tension—as John Turl points out when he writes that, "…whether or not we can postulate a reasonable method of interaction, for Christians the basic datum is that pure spirit can interact with matter." (2010) Turl offers the following examples:

- o God, who is spirit, created the universe, which is matter (John. 4:24; 1:3).
- o Angels have communicated with humans (Hebrews.1:14; Luke 1:13,28).
- o The Holy Spirit affects human minds (John. 14:26; 16:8)

In his conclusion Turl points out the following: "It seems difficult if not impossible to construct a non-reductive monism; reductive monism seems unacceptable philosophically and theologically.

Scripture does not favor monism in preference to a dualistic account of man. It is not necessary to assume that physics is hostile to the existence of an ontological soul."

From a theistic perspective, Turl's conclusion is entirely reasonable—and indeed plausible. This may seem somewhat of a paradoxical state of affairs as we appear to be referring to both a process of evolution that is unguided and a deity that is able, in ways indiscernible to any sophisticated microscope, to somehow, within the biological process, bring about changes in line with some teleological objectives. The point here is that there are outcomes that may be predicted and outcomes that may not.

Even if such a world as ours has arisen via an evolutionary process: Would it 'really' have arisen through an unguided natural process? i.e. a process that could guarantee nothing more than the survival of the 'best adapted biological systems'—however these 'systems' may 'turnout'. One can imagine though that, should a God-ordained process begin again, it would produce exactly the same results—precisely because it is a part of the Telos of the mind of God—the Goal of Creation.

Should God so work within the Cosmos it has to be admitted that there is little evidence of God 'actively' pursuing paths that ease the suffering of the 'products' of such a state of affairs. However, should the evolutionary process have been left completely to its 'own devices', there would be no guarantee of a good outcome—especially regarding the free-will choices of lesser beings—and the emergence of the imago Dei—the incarnation, the victory of the Son of God over these principalities and powers. Moreover, it is also the case that Scripture offers a better outcome than the predictions of speculative (theoretical) physics: either 'the big crunch' or the 'big freeze'—an outcome that God has purposed from before the creation of the world—even the Telos of God.

Creaturely Flourishing

In his book, The Groaning of Creation, Christopher Southgate gives much attention to the hope of a future state of affairs (heaven) where creatures that have, through the effects of predation, etc. have not been able to flourish—to 'fully self', in other words to have had the best of possible 'life-experience'. Whether or not this failure to 'fully self' is a question of moral failure on God's part or of the necessary consequences of Natural Selection—or both— it does require qualification—as the alleged moral failure of God is at the center of the Problem of Evil—both evidential and philosophical.

Marilyn McCord Adams says that to argue for the falsity of Christianity on the grounds that the existence of an omnipotent, omniscient, pleasure-maximiser is incompossible with a world such as ours, because Christians [at least those taking the Bible seriously] have never believed that God was such a 'pleasure-maximiser' anyway. (1999). It is a question of whether the purpose of life is to provide what some philosophers describe as 'a good thing' and not the opposite—so that the end of this 'good thing' isn't an issue—excepting when that 'experience' is neither good or fully experienced. It was William A. Rowe who argued that— should there be one example of an opposite experience to 'the good'—either for humankind or for animals—whether sentient or otherwise--then the claim for the existence of 'the deity' is but a fabrication. Much has been written in response to Rowe; his view—that creatures with high order consciousness (at least) should have a positive experience of 'life'—the implication being that should that not be the case then we can rule out any notion of benevolence. There is, of course, much more to Rowe's views than the above caricature—but even in its philosophical sophistication—it is not sufficient enough of an argument to deny the existence of God, i.e. the God of The Judeo/Christian Scriptures—particularly as this God is not some kind of divine 'pleasure-maximiser'

Thomas Aquinas concludes that the word 'evil' does not signify any essence, form or substance. Evil, he advocates, can only be described as an 'absence of goodness'. Anything that lacks 'goodness' can, according to Aquinas, be described as 'evil', which, for Aquinas, simply means less than good. God, according to Aquinas, did not, and could not have created anything less than good. Aquinas concludes that the word 'evil' does not signify any essence, form or substance. Evil, he advocates, can only be described as an 'absence of goodness'. Anything that lacks 'goodness' can, according to Aquinas, be described as 'evil', which, for Aquinas, simply means less than good. God, according to Aquinas, did not, and could not have created anything less than good. If it is the case that, as Aquinas maintains and as I argue in this book: that which God creates is 'GOOD'. This is not to be confused with perfect—especially as the notion of perfection is a manmade construct —a comparison with other states of existence and of experience. What God does is, de facto, The Good. (Aquinas, 2003)

With regards to flourishing—i.e. 'to grow or develop successfully'—it is the case that, in this world, things, so often, do not either 'grow or flourish'—and even the things that flourish and grow--eventually fall fowl of the physical laws of the universe— and they perish or decay. The question is: Can this state of affairs bring about a charge of failure or ineptitude on behalf of the Creator? Would it be acceptable therefore to accuse God of injustice? Indeed, can God be accused of moral failure? Accusations against God that are based on the notion of God's apparent [moral] failure to produce a world in which 'Human Rights' are being fulfilled, and in which Southgate's 'Creaturely Selfing' is a given, seem to ignore the fact that the [present] created order is the way it is because of the functioning of its physical laws. There are, of course, other factors and influences— not least the anthropic influence.

However, is it really God's sole responsibility to provide the best of possible life-experiences for all of the created order? Of course, should it be the case that God has no influence whatsoever regarding the creative state of affairs that produce much of the misery experienced by both animals and humans alike then we may well conclude that God is an 'under achiever'. However, the notion that GOD has to bring about a state of affairs in which creatures can 'sail through life'—experiencing the best of possible outcomes whilst avoiding the less than popular experiences is based on the rather anthropomorphic assumption that even none-sentient life forms should realise any kind of life-experience that would warrant a more wholesome 're-run' of that 'experience'— without the predation etc. That God, whilst having to be, from this perspective, the 'pleasure maximiser' rather than the 'pain condoner', has some kind of moral responsibility to produce the best of possible experience for every creature in the history of the biosphere is, obviously, based on a false assumption. Moreover, regarding the thumb-endowed creatures with the proclivity to live life according to their own self-directed desires—their having the best of possible future experience whilst living this life as if there were, in existence, no such 'benefactor' seems to be a somewhat unreasonable notion. "And he who was seated on the throne said, 'Behold, I am making all things new.' Also he said, 'Write these things down, for these words are trustworthy and true." Revelation 21:5

I shall end this section with the words of C.S.Lewis as written in his classic apologetic work 'The Problem of Pain':

> There is a kindness in love but love and kindness are not coterminous, and when kindness is separated from the other elements of love, it involves a certain fundamental indifference to its object, and even something like contempt of it. Kindness consents very readily to the removal of its object—we have all met people whose kindness to animals is constantly leading them to kill animals lest they should suffer....Kindness, merely as such, cares not whether its object becomes good or bad, provided that it only escapes suffering. If God is Love, he is, by definition, something more than mere kindness. And it appears, from all the records, that though He has often rebuked us and condemned us, He has never regarded us with contempt. He has paid us the intolerable compliment of loving us, in the deepest, most tragic, most inexorable sense. (Lewis, 1996)

Is Heaven a Necessary World?

It seems to me that there is far too much focus on acquiescing to the materialist agenda—so much so that any argument, biblical or otherwise, that suggests that any idea of 'heaven' has, indeed, to be brought down to the level of 'The Material' i.e. the material that science is, presently, familiar with, as the only option open to God.

Having discussed various insights into the redemptive possibilities offered by some scientists and theologians, engaging in what may be described as eschatological conjecture, Christopher Southgate underlines his view that, since this world is the world the God of 'all creativity and all compassion' chose for the creation of carbon-based-life-forms, we must presume therefore that there was no other option—that, though heaven can eternally preserve all of the creatures (over time—that have ever existed) in an environment that is suffering-free—it could not give rise to them in the first place. In other words: without such a (protracted) process these creatures (every single one of them) could not have existed. The likelyhodd of this being the case, raises the obvious question regarding God's diffidence/reluctance in producing a better environment. If an omnipotent God could have, initially, created heaven, why did God not do so?

As Michael Lloyd et al (Lloyd, 2018) have made clear; it is not sufficient to avoid the question—or to offer a solely eschatological defence—as such defences, in their desire for scientific/ philosophical acceptance, tend to be 'anti-Christian'. In other words—the defence/theodicy that does not have Scripture as its prime source (its raison d'être) is, de facto, deficient. Here, Southgate offers a clear but 'challenging' explanation. He suggests that though heaven can eternally preserve the 'selves' (in 'a new, heaven and new earth', environment) 'Heaven' cannot give rise to the carbon-based-life-forms that evolution has produced.

Ergo, the 4 billion years or so of evolutionary development has been a necessary state of affairs. The implications with this reasoning (from a theistic perspective) are challenging to say the least. And, even if we were to allow for the commonly held belief that evolution was its own 'master'—that it is the 'unguided hand' of a naturally selective process that gives rise to all that is biological (even cosmological)—it makes no sense to talk about goals—even goals that God may have hope to, somehow, accomplish—unless the state of 'being in #heaven' is an altogether different state of affairs; though this, I hasten to add, could not, *a facie eius*, explain how the creator could have anticipated an 'outcome'—though it could beimagined that, as God is outside of the space-time continuum, God would know 'the end from the beginning' and 'possibly' be satisfied with the outcome:

> …declaring the end from the beginning and from ancient times things not yet done, saying, 'My counsel shall stand, and I will accomplish all my purpose,'… (Isaiah 46:10).

The above quote from Isaiah is not, of course, a support text for naturalistic evolution—it is, rather, a confirmation of the sovereignty of God. The argument I am putting forward in this book is that for God's [sovereign] outcomes (as revealed in Scripture) to realise, there has to be a 'blue-print' for the emergence/ creation of mankind (imago Dei) as the 'vessel made of clay'—fit for the Spirit of God (Swinburne, 1997).

This, I suggest, rules out the possibility that God should 'play dice with the universe'—but rather that God intentionally brought about the creation of our species—a species that was 'fit for the purposes of God'.

In his book entitled: 'Improbable Destinies: How Predictable is Evolution?', biology professor Jonathan Losos argues that evolution is not random but that it "…restricts the way that species can evolve, often constraining them to adapt in the same way when facing similar environmental circumstances.". (2017) Losos though is not suggesting that there is any 'design' in evolution but he does suggest that "If any countless number of events had occurred differently in the past Homo sapiens would not have evolved. We were far from inevitable and are lucky to be here—fortunate that events happened as they did." So, is this a question of the 'unseen hand' of a purely natural process or the unseen hand of the invisible God? Of course not all Biology Professors agree—depending on their differing 'World Views'.

In his 2017 book: "Purpose & Desire: "What makes something alive and why Modern Darwinism has failed to explain it?". Biology Professor J. Scott Turner asks what it is that actually drives evolution forward: "Is it the tokens of memory that force life into an uncertain pushing there to stand or die? Or is it a forward looking intentionality that strides confidently into the future, dragging the memory tokens along in its wake, intending to stand rather than simply to die?" Turner answers his own questions with an affirmative that, as far as he is concerned, moves the debate along from purposelessness to what he refers to as 'purpose and desire':

> No longer are we stuck in the bleak landscape of the Four Horsemen of the 'Evo-calypse', where there is no purpose, no desire, no intention—only the indifferent churning of a machine. From where we stand now, we can at least begin to see a landscape where those essential attributes of life purposefulness, striving, desire, intentionality, intelligence—can once again reenchant our understanding of life and of everything about it, including its evolution. (Turner, 2017)

For the sake of the argument here, the necessary constituents for God's planned intentions can be listed under the following brief headings:

a) The 'Telos' of [God] through a 'directional' evolutionary process.

b) The existence of the Second Law of Thermodynamics—allowing for the effects of entropy—for its necessary consequences: Life and Death.

c) The notion of Free-Will, as (particularly) expressed in the lives and experience of the species that Scripture describes as being made in the image of God (imago Dei).

d) The physical appearance (incarnation), life, suffering, death and resurrection of the second person of the Trinity: Jesus Christ.

e) The existence of a place that we may call Heaven but that isn't governed by the current physical laws.

Regarding the 4 billion-year-biological-evolutionary-state-of-affairs, Adrian Hough (2010) offers some interesting and useful insights—perceptions that are germane to the argument here. Hough states that, in more scientific terms, we are able to say that the increase in entropy or disorder (which is, at least 'presently' a fundamental characteristic of the universe) is the cause of suffering and of death. Hough adds to this by asking whether the cross of Christ can also be seen as God accepting the consequences of the Second Law?

Though God, I believe, would not shrink from taking whatever responsibility 'is God's', I do not accept the argument that offers the cross of Christ as some kind of 'self-punishment' for God's own failure to produce a better outcome—in particular for the, presumed, billions of years of suffering 'meted out' by Natural Selection; though I do take seriously the notion that this 'silent' universe somehow echoes the cry of the 'Crucified [Son] of God'. It is in this sense that the universe is cruciform, for how could the sacrifice of God the Son not reverberate throughout space-time. The apostle Paul eloquently states:

> For from him and through him and for him are all things.
> To him be the glory forever! Amen. (Romans 11:36)

God, I maintain, is not guilty of producing a world that could have been otherwise created; this world is the only possible world that is fit for the purposes of God—despite any attempt by 'deviance' to bring about another outcome. It is also the world that God intended to create, and it is in this world, and no other, that the Problem of Evil has been dealt its death blow. This world is the best possible world—in which the consequences that Hough refers to can also obtain. Yet it is also the world in which 'The Son of God' can take on himself the sins of the world—of the flesh and of the devil aka 'the satan'. It is in this world that God allows the results of free-will to have, seemingly, free-reign; yet it is, most likely not, a world out of which can arise a different state of affairs—a world wherein the Second Law must have a somewhat different functionality i.e. Surely 'this world'—this 'new heaven and earth' has to be somewhat different:

> Then I saw a new heaven and a new earth, for the first
> heaven and the first earth had passed away,… (Revelation
> 21:1)

Hough says that what is clear from the present consideration is that:

> … the Second Law of Thermodynamics leads us to a
> grander vision of God if our vision of God begins with the

assumption that Jesus Christ rose from the dead and that God wills the renewal of His creation…If we consider the way in which the universe works, then it is clear that God has in some sense to be beyond the universe.

Key to the argument in this book is that this World Order (since its genesis) can be described in terms of its being the only possible world in which all that God has ordained may take place. It is this present world—with both its values and disvalues—a world that allows for the worst of possible suffering and deprivation—a world in which the malignant effects of the fallen natures of both angels and men seem to prevail. It is this world as—with no other that allows for 'the good, the bad and the ugly'—a world in which the created order may demonstrate (unexplained) altruism, acts of compassion, love and self-sacrifice. Moreover, it is this world that is subject to the effects of particular laws that, humans at least, have no means of controlling or of changing. This is not to say that mankind can effect no change whatsoever, but that it would not be possible for mankind, per se, to create a heaven on earth or to change the prevailing cosmological state of affairs—though it is reasonable to expect creatures that were 'there' at the beginning of creation—that were even agents of the creator to effect considerable change to the biosphere, i.e. agents that 'were cast out of heaven' into a place in which they were unable to escape their destiny—yet 'challenge' the divine will and thereafter to bring about the most heinous of circumstances.

It is, though, the Triune God that promises a better state of affairs—an eschatological fulfilment of God's ultimate purposes for his creation—a creation that bears the scars of the 'Crucified God' (Moltmann, 1993) Theologian Sam Storms writes that:

> …the unfolding fulfilment of God's promises may be seen in terms of what Geerhardus Vos called a 'binary configuration'. That is to say, human history reflects a tension between what was accomplished at the first advent of Christ and what awaits consummation at the second. (Storms, 2013)

Christopher Southgate refers to the insights of the physicist and theologian R.J.Russell who sees the resurrection of Jesus Christ as the beginning of a final act that will transform the character of creation'—adding that "The long sweep of evolution may not only suggest an unfinished and continuing divine creation but even more radically a creation whose theological status as 'good' may be fully realised only in the eschatological future." (2008) I agree with Russell, it is 'the resurrection' that gives a clue to 'The Victory of God'—rather any other speculative notions of a 'redeemed earth,' Indeed, 'The Resurrection of The Son of God' was that which heralded a 'New Order'—an order in which the entropic principle no longer dictates outcomes. Of course, it may be the case that God renews the present cosmos rather than destroy the existing and replace it with a 'new and improved model'.

However, if God has needed billions of years to produce a better model, it may be the case that God is not omnipotent at all but that, with GOD it is more to do with limited resources and ability than with omniscience and sovereignty.

While having sympathy with the opinions of Southgate and Russell—vis a vis their view that creation's good status may be 'identified' as being good only at the eschaton; I do not think it at all necessary to deny 'the creation' its 'good' status at any time in its history; for the creation has been good from its genesis and it shall remain good throughout eternity—whatever the intrusion. Moreover, it is, I suggest, a mistake to base one's reading of all that 'Scripture' promises (at the eschaton) solely on an evolutionary/material/reclaimed model of what 'New Heavens and a New Earth' might look like—an idea aided and abetted by a functional interpretation of what it means to be 'made in the image of God' (imago Dei). That is not to say that there is any desire to detract from what may be described as the 'governance of humanity' but, rather, that governance is not mankind's only purpose.

I have throughout this book, argued that the creation is good—good in terms of it being good and not evil. I have maintained that the creation is as it is because, mostly, its evolutionary process has been a necessary state of affairs rather than the product of an amorphous deity or of [mere] elemental forces. I have said that creation's evolution coalesces with the purposes (telos) of a God who is personal—a determinate entity rather than a force that defies description—sitting more comfortably with current trends in philosophical theology. I have further argued that God, that is, The God of Scripture, is both sovereign and benevolent. Moreover, I have said that rather than being the absolute product of a deficient deity or a defiant adversary (though it is most likely the case that there has been significant 'tinkering') the creation is as it is because it has been a necessary state of affairs and that (though considered less than satisfactory by created beings) it is indeed an essential state of affairs. Indeed it shall be the case (at the eschaton) that the Sovereign God of the universe will bring deliverance for those longing, as the apostle Paul intimates in his letter to the Christians in Rome, "…for the revealing of the sons of God." (Romans 8:19)

> My Father's house has many rooms; if that were not so, would I have told you that I am going there to prepare a place for you? And if I go and prepare a place for you, I will come back and take you to be with me that you also may be where I am. (John 14:2,3)

PART5

TELOS

Only Such a World

It stands to reason that if God were 'able' (due to God's omnipotence) to create a world without the deleterious effects of entropy, then it is reasonable to ask why it is God may not have taken this direction when working out his grand plan for the creation of the universe. Could God have not produced a better environment than planet earth so that there was less likelihood of, at least, natural disasters? The answer is, unequivocally in the negative; and it is for this reason: This universal system is not merely the best of all possible systems conducive to the formation of biological life—life in all its vulnerability. It is more crucially, the only system that would have allowed for God to deal with the 'Universal' Problem of Evil: to prepare a 'biological pathway' for the arrival of mankind, and therefore the possibility of the incarnation of the second person of the Trinity, and henceforth the redemption of creation through the Cross of Christ.

That the incarnation, resurrection and ascension of the second Person of the Trinity are significant events is beyond doubt. However, what may not be so readily observable (unless seen through the lens of theoretical physics—into the 'world' of parallel universes), is the possibility that the new world order (new heavens and new earth) may already exist—having been developing in tandem with the 'known world'. What I am suggesting is that this 'New World' is where Christ (and, possibly many other such bodies) dwell at present--for there is at least one resurrected body in another 'place'. That this is somehow synonymous with that which will appear from 'heaven'—as the vision of John records ("And I saw the holy city, new Jerusalem, coming down out of heaven from God, prepared as a bride adorned for her husband." Revelation 21:2) is a possibility. It is appreciated however that this particular passage refers to 'the Church'. But it also gives detail of this 'Holy City'.

J.J. Wilson (2013) describes the 'new heavens and new earth' as: "…not a second creation or a simple restoration of the first heaven and earth; it is the redemption of creation for its telos [that] takes place in Jesus Christ. The blessedness of the 'beatitudes' is now fulfilled in the new creation."

Cambridge paleontologist and evolutionary biologist, Simon Conway Morris (2003) refers to the significance of the evolution of humans, or something very closely related: "We may be unique, but paradoxically those properties that define our uniqueness can still be inherent in the evolutionary process. In other words, if we humans had not evolved then something more or less identical would have emerged sooner or later." Whatever the 'actuality' of the evolutionary process, mankind's place in the 'developing scale of events' has, it seems, been inevitable and is exceptional within the created order. Evolution was given, seemingly, a clear direction—there was, what may be considered, a 'blueprint' for the process. Oxford (Thomas Aquinas) Theologian, William Carroll (quoting various sources) succinctly outlines his view of the theistic implications within the biological process:

> Although chance events are frequent and important in biological evolution, rendering its actual course indeterminate or unpredictable in exact outcome from any particular stage, these events and their short and long-term effects—whether they be of point mutations at the level of molecular DNA, or the impact of a meteorite—are always within a context of regularities, constraints, and possibilities. Thus, to refer to such events as 'pure chance' or to assert blithely that evolution proceeds by purely chance events is much less than a precise description of this source of unpredictability in biological evolution…

Furthermore, even though the contemporary natural sciences often seek to discover efficient causes without reference to purposes (final causes), any ordering of efficient causes and their effects implicitly acknowledges and presupposes that the efficient causes and the processes which embody them are directed towards the realisation of certain specific types of ends. Efficient causes always have certain specifiable effects. (2000)

The point being made in the above quote is that an omnipotent God can bring order out of chaos or order out of what may appear to be undirected evolutionary processes. However one discerns the means through which the God of the Judeo/Christian Scriptures 'directs' creative processes—we 'dare say' that Earth is the 'blue sphere' that God had prepared for the arrival of Homo sapiens[58] and for such an event as the incarnation of Christ and the Annunciation of 'Release for the Captives' (Isaiah 42:7). As has been previously argued this world is the best possible world, in which there could have arisen intelligent carbon-based life forms.

---

[58] William Stone (2014,pp.53-81) suggests that Adam could be placed at the route of the Homo erectus/ergaster to Homo sapiens lineage around .8 million years ago. Stone qualifies this by adding that his conclusion was somewhat contingent on the acceptance of a number of presuppositions that were "bound up with current paleoanthropological models." Stone commented that he had not addressed the wider issues of relating the 'human' fossil record to the biblical narrative, which is something of particular importance. Stone's is a suggestion — though there is continual debate and 'much returning to the drawing board'-Circa 2015...

Indeed, as Michael Murray (2008) points out, we have no knowledge of any other such worlds in which biological evolution as we know it could succeed.

Regarding the creation of this world the Genesis text states: "God saw everything he had made and it was very good". (1:31). God sustains the world as well as the universe within the boundaries[59] God has set for it. According to the Genesis text, the creative results were not only good but they were 'very good'; 'everything had gone to plan'; the result being that it was 'very good'. There followed, what appeared to be, a 'dark side' to the process[60]—that of the effects of the negative side of the Second Law of Thermodynamics—the increase of entropy that, some argue, ensured the likelihood of the evolutionary process. However, what may appear to some observers to be the dark side of the laws of physics need be nothing of the sort. Rather, the laws, as ordained by the creator, were a necessary ingredient for the creation and development of carbon-based life—culminating in the 'late' arrival of the image bearers of God. It is by the universal laws of physics that the Triune God is able to bring about ultimate

---

[59] What is meant by 'boundaries' is the limits that God may have preordained for the development of his creation both cosmological [in terms of the expansion of the universe] and biological, in terms of God's restrictions on the limits of evolutionary development, as well as God's prohibitions on any undesired interference to that development—by any created beings—humans or otherwise.]

[60] "..the Second Law taken in isolation leads us to predict a future (which is one) of disorder and ultimate decay..." (Hough 2010, 143)

justice. God, in Christ, is able to give of himself on the cross so that there could be resolution and reconciliation.

With reference to the efficacy of the Cross of Christ the apostle Paul states that:

> …while we were enemies we were reconciled to God by the death of his Son, much more, now that we are reconciled, shall we be saved by his life. More than that, we also rejoice in God through our Lord Jesus Christ, through whom we have now received reconciliation. (Romans 5:10)

Christ has dealt with the problem of evil through his death on the cross. The cross is the ultimate act of justice through which God reconciles a fallen world to himself—thus realizing the cosmos from its bondage and decay. The Apostle Paul states that "…if righteousness were through the law, then Christ died for no purpose." (Galatians 2:21) The acceptance of God's offer of unconditional forgiveness is a matter of grace but it is also a matter of the heart as is made clear in Romans 10:9:

> If you confess with your mouth that Jesus is Lord and believe in your heart that God raised him from the dead, you will be saved.

Rapprochement and Grace work together—the critical point is that this momentous act of sacrifice and of reconciliation is, according to Scripture, found in Christ alone (Acts 4:12).

My argument in this book is that any kinds of harms—whether the results of predation, parasitism and plague or the consequence of plate tectonic movement etc. can be regarded as consequences of, mostly, a necessary-natural-state-of-affairs. However, the 'evil' that does manifest itself within the world is far from natural, it is rather the result of deviancy within the minds and wills of both terrestrial and extra-terrestrial beings—ergo it is 'moral' rather than natural, and it manifests itself in every hideous shape and form. It is this 'angelic moral deviancy' and resultant rebellion that the Creator God considered before the initiation of the creation ex nihilo—'omniscience' being a key factor to the knowledge required by God to outmaneuver the enemies of God. Of course to argue that God exists let alone having 'powerful' extra-terrestrial bi-corporeal enemies (though the 'pen' may be considered more powerful than the sword), for the materialist a matter of ridicule— but no less so than for the notion of luck i.e. the roll of the dice as in the argument offered by materialists.

A prominent atheist back in the 1990s was asked whether life (in all of its amazing diversity) came about by chance. His answer, in short, was that the chances of this happening would be like throwing dice into the air a thousand times and getting a six every time—'impossible!' But, the luminary added, should there be a degree of luck along the 'naturally selected pathway' (my words) then anything is possible. What is impossible, from this 'belief system' aka 'World View' is that there may be in existence anything other than the products of accidental cause and effect—whether in our galaxy or elsewhere. The idea being that, as life started here by chance, one would expect it to have occurred elsewhere. The Search Continues…

The argument here is that it is God alone who has the wherewithal to bring about and to sustain a biosphere teaming with life and purpose. From the perspective of the materialist everything is perfectly natural—yet there can, in reality, be neither purpose or design—from this 'chance & necessity perspective' no 'Grand Design'. Yet, beneath the veneer of, what may be considered, chance and necessity, there lay a deeper reality over time—an unfurling of the telos of God.

Perhaps it was the 'unfurling' of God's plans for creation that enabled/allowed the angels' insight into the (perceived) plans and purposes of God. Whatever the truth, the fallen angels could not have fully comprehended the plans and purposes of God—plans that were to bring about the redemption of a cosmos tainted by the actions and interventions of deviants. It would be mistaken to conclude that any such rebellion from angels would have been due to envy regarding the creation/emergence of Homo sapiens from 'out of' any evolutionary process—for there would have been 'little' difference between these creatures and any other 'genetically related' species that inhabited the planet at this time. However, should there be more to the 'thumb endowed creature than mere 'sapience'—something other than materialistic notions of reality will allow—then there might well be a clue as to their unhappy state.

Scripture suggests (Hebrews 2:7-9) that humankind were made a little lower than the angels—and that God 'crowned them with glory and honor—putting everything under their feet.' The idea that mere 'sapience' would have been enough to inscite a rebellion of this magnitude makes little sense. However, should these creatures have had the potential for something far greater than sapience, this would be a different matter (no pun intended) altogether. Indeed, the idea of mankind as being nothing other than the 'fine end' of an evolutionary process makes little sense—at least for those of us who have not been blinded by a materialistic world-view that disallows any ideas that conflict with the notion of a 'materially driven' unified theory of everything. According to Scripture, it is the incarnation, the death, the resurrection into 'new life' of the one in whom and through whom 'the world was created'—and is 'held together'. It is this 'divine intrusion' into the materialist's 'world view' that human reason and even scientific-driven-theology casts aside in its quest for the elusive grand theory of everything or its acquiescence to the transience of ideas that fit neatly within the evolutionary paradigm.

> He is the image of the invisible God, the firstborn of all
> creation. For by him all things were created, in heaven and
> on earth, visible and invisible, whether thrones
> or dominions or rulers or authorities—all things were

created through him and for him. And he is before all things, and in him all things hold together. And he is the head of the body, the church. He is the beginning, the firstborn from the dead, that in everything he might be preeminent. For in him all the fullness of God was pleased to dwell, and through him to reconcile to himself all things, whether on earth or in heaven, making peace by the blood of his cross. (Colossians 1:15-20 ESV)

It is, I suggest, likely that the extra-terrestrial deviants (fallen angels) would have been ignorant of God's plans and intentions for the redemption of the 'world':

For God so loved the world, that he gave his only Son, that whoever believes in him should not perish but have eternal life. For God did not send his Son into the world to condemn the world, but in order that the world might be saved through him. Whoever believes in him is not condemned, but whoever does not believe is condemned already, because he has not believed in the name of the only Son of God. And this is the judgment: the light has come into the world, and people loved the darkness rather than the light because their works were evil. (John 3:16-19)

Should these august creatures have known, they would not have allowed such a state of affairs to obtain—for it would, eventually, bring about their demise and to release the captives from the bondage and decay that God has allowed—and that the present physical laws make possible. If this sounds a little like 'Star Wars', it is also ***similar to that*** which Gregory Boyd suggests in the following:

> The view that evil spirits are largely responsible for 'natural' evil has been suggested throughout church history…But due to the influence of Augustine's blueprint model of divine providence, this insight was rarely considered the ultimate explanation for 'natural' evil, as it was before Augustine. The assumption was that everything that demons do somehow fits in with God's meticulous plan for world history. Because of this, 'natural' evil has generally been regarded as a problem of understanding God's providence, not an issue of spiritual warfare…Modern perspectives on 'natural' evil have drifted even further from the warfare perspective and the post-apostolic church. Under the influence of Enlightenment naturalism, rationalism and biblical criticism, the very notion of evil spirits influencing the physical world became (and continues to be) problematic. Physical laws became the ultimate explanation for everything in the physical world. (2001)

Contrary to Boyd's view, my view is that God is indeed sovereign but also that Fallen Angels have considerable influence within the seen and the unseen realms. This, I am convinced is not a contradiction—neither is it a deviation from my belief in the Sovereignty of God.

The Goal of Creation

It will be apparent from what I have written previously, that though I appreciate some of the ideas that other Bible-believing theologians offer I most definitely do not hold a view that denigrates—or even lessens the attributes of God, i.e. my views differ somewhat from the opinions of Open Theists.

Scripture attests to the incarnational objectives of the second person of the Trinity. Andrew Trotter (1997) refers to the importance of eschatology as recorded in the letter to the Hebrews—pointing out that the prologue catalogues what had happened in Christ, "… in a historical progression of events moving from his role as Creator to Redeemer to heavenly intermediary for his people." .

> …to which of the angels has he (God) ever said, 'Sit at my right hand until I make your enemies a footstool for your feet.'(Christ) …for a little while made a little lower than the angels…..crowned with glory and honor because of the suffering of death, so that by the grace of God he might taste death for everyone…that through death he might destroy the one who has the power of death, that is, the devil. (Hebrews 1:13; 2:7,14).

The irony is that God, by allowing for the physical laws that bring about what may be considered the worst possible state of affairs, actually allows for the best possible state of affairs to obtain— God's victory over the enemies of God—and of sin and death.

Colin Dye (Dye, 2013) refers to Genesis 3:14&15 as the first glimpse of the gospel, the foreshadowing of the cross— pointing specifically to the Victory of God over that which is Evil. Indeed, "The Lord said to the serpent and her offspring; 'Because you have done this, cursed are you above all livestock and above all beasts of the field: on your belly, you shall go, and dust you shall eat all the days of your life. I will put enmity between you and the woman, and between your offspring, and her offspring; he shall bruise your head, and you shall bruise his heel.'"Genesis 3:14,15 (ESV) "This first prediction of triumph identified the woman's seed, or offspring, as the one who would be ultimately victorious. It was later revealed to the prophets that this 'seed' would be the Messiah, the Christos or 'Anointed Man', who would establish God's righteous rule and eradicate evil." (2013)

Regarding the incarnation Adrio König (1989) points out that when the apostle Paul states that 'all things are created for Christ' (Colossians 1:16), "...here we have the goal of creation. Creation is aimed toward Christ as its target; it moves toward him, and in him, it will reach its goal.[61]Ivor Davidson (2011) refers to God's 'end designs' when he says that "The God who saves is the God who is creator, sustainer, redeemer and perfecter of all things, the one who elects to enter into irrevocable union with materiality, whose Spirit animates all life, and who surely has purposes for all that he has made. While there is much that we cannot say about the details of what this entails eschatologically, God, it seems, intends that not just humans but creatures of all kinds should attain the glory of freedom and fulfilment in relation to their creator. Jonathan R. Wilson (2013) states that it is when Christians progress a Trinitarian doctrine of creation (in what Wilson refers to as "being in dialectic with redemption") it is 'then' that they have good news for their interlocutors—indeed for society. Given our convictions about creation…we may know that the refusal to believe in Christ as the telos of the universe will lead to despair even as society develops strategies, practices and products to ameliorate and manage the despair.

> He is the image of the invisible God, the firstborn of all creation. For by him all things were created, in heaven and on earth, visible and invisible, whether thrones or dominions or rulers or authorities—all things were

---

[61] König points out that there is no contradiction between this and such statements as Romans 11:36 and Hebrews 2:10 where we read that God (the Father) is the purpose of creation—for there is no disunity between Father and Son. The same applies to Hebrews 2:10 and also to Colossians 1:16.

created through him and for him. And he is before all things, and in him, all things hold together. And he is the head of the body, the church. He is the beginning, the firstborn from the dead, that in everything he might be preeminent. For in him all the fullness of God was pleased to dwell, and through him to reconcile to himself all things, whether on earth or in heaven, making peace by the blood of his cross. (Colossians 1:15-20)

N.T.Wright refers to the above passage from Paul's letter to the Colossians as, "...a spectacular early Christian poem [which] places Jesus' resurrection (1:18) in parallel with the creation of the world (1:15), seeing it as the ground and origin of what the creator has now accomplished and is now implementing, namely the reconciliation of all things to him." (2003) Wright's conviction that the very shape of the poem insists that Jesus' resurrection, as a one-off event, is an act not of the elimination of the original creation but of its fulfilment fits in with the argument here. Wright's conclusion that, "...the one through whom all things were made in the first place; the one through whom all things cohere; the one in and through all things are now brought into a new relationship with the creator God and with one another.." coheres with my argument: The eternal Son of God—through his life, death and resurrection reconciled all things to himself. " He [God] disarmed the rulers and authorities and put them to open shame, by triumphing over them in him [Christ]." (Colossians 2:15)

The Justice of God

Without penalty any notion of law is meaningless. Any action by agents with the capacity 'to will to choose' brings with it the consequences of that action. Peter Lowman (2002) says, "… to the biblical worldview, the world as a whole was condemned to purposelessness by the first humans' assertion of independence from God that we call The Fall. The results were meaninglessness—futility." This 'one act of rebellion' (as reported in Genesis 3) was, de facto, the precursor to both condemnation and intervention—God's intervention being particularly delineated in Genesis 2 and 3 where the text refers to: 'a loss of life potential' (2:17); 'increased pain awareness' (3:16); 'a radical change in the environs' (3:17-19), and the loss of access to the 'tree', which is, in some way analogous of 'the source of the sustenance of life' (3:23,24) . However, this 'one' act of rebellion by the 'Adamic' pair was not the source of the Problem of Evil, it was instead the outworking of the revolution of angels (affecting/infecting the creature made in the image of God) that had taken place 'prior' to the creation of the physical universe[62]. Yet it was within this material universe (within the constraints allowed by the physical

---

[62] 'Events' <u>prior to the beginning of the space/time continuum</u> are not events that can be measured as such. However, the need for intelligible communication dictates the use of time words and of tenses; consequently, when we refer to an authentic occurrence before the creation of the Universe there is little option but to use such language.

laws that God had ordained) that the effects of these laws (outside of the garden) had already been made manifest. It was to the outside of this 'Eden'—this 'sacred place' (Walton 2009)—that the first pair would have been expelled. As with the angels who were cast out of heaven, so the man and woman were thrown out of Eden not because they had the will to choose but that they decided to oppose God—to abjure from loving and serving and enjoying the presence of their creator God. The 'casting out' of the Adamic pair (Genesis 3:22&23), and the casting down of Satan and his angels (Revelation 12:7-12; Luke 10:18) entailed banishment and exile; for the imago Dei, this meant expulsion from the paradise— from the potential for life in all its fullness. Moreover, the fallen angels', banishment from the presence of God—into an environment from which there would be no exit (Jude 13; Revelation 20).

Could it be the case that these creatures, having been cast out of heaven, infecting both the biosphere and their own self[s]— were, as fallen angels, lesser beings with diminished powers—in some way subject to the laws of physics? We can but speculate. They, however, have continued to war against the creation that God had declared good.

Beyond Mere-Metaphysics

An effect is brought about by a cause. In other words 'events' occur as the result of other events or ideas; events then (physical or otherwise) are brought about by an event or set of circumstances:

> In creating the world, God says one thing then another,
> building on what he has just said and done. This
> progression has an inherent logic because the effect of one
> word depends logically on the prior effect of others (e.g.
> the creation of fish presupposes the creation of water).
> (Dembski, 2009)

In other words 'the order of creation'

Dembski refers to this 'order of creation.' as 'history from the vantage point of divine intention and action.' The divine intentions and actions being, logically, prior to others. This 'logical priority' rather than 'temporal priority' defines history for God. Dembski makes an important distinction between events brought about by 'chance & necessity' and events that are decreed by the will of the God of Creation. Dembski points out that 'Natural History' confines history to space-time events and sees the logic of history as determined entirely by physical causality, i.e. natural causation. Dembski makes the observation (too easily overlooked by theologians and other interested parties) that the distinction between the order of creation and natural history reflects a fundamental distinction regarding the nature of time. It is this distinction that Dembski focuses on in his observations regarding the actions of the Sovereign God of the Universe and the events otherwise accredited to nature.

Dembski, notes that 'in the real world' there are no causally isolated events. Everything hangs together with everything else. The slightest change in one thing changes everything. In his chapter entitled 'Chronos & Kairos, Dembski gives good reasons why it is reasonable to suppose that God can act across time—or as he expresses 'transtemporally'. Dembski points out that in English we only have the one word for 'time whereas New Testament Greek has two, Chronos & Kairos.

> Chronos denotes mere duration, but Kairos denotes time with a purpose—especially 'a divine purpose.' e.g.; 'It is not yet'—in Other words the time has not yet come…The visible realm operates according to Chronos (the simple passage of time). But the invisible realm, in which God resides, operates according to Kairos, the ordering of reality according to divine purposes. (Dembski, 2009)

There is, 'naturally', a problem with the idea of God acting transtemporally. The very idea is, from an evolutionary perspective (of whatever shade) preposterous. There is indeed a perceived problem—but not in the least from a biblical perspective. This perceived problem arises particularly if there is any hint of anthropomorphism. Dembski affirms that this is, without doubt, the case and states that 'a kairological interpretation of the six days of creation is unashamedly anthropomorphic'—moreover Genesis unequivocally teaches that 'humans are the end of creation.' Dembski opines that even though God has granted the world a measure of 'natural autonomy', the world's autonomy is not absolute:

> Just as an orchestra needs the conductor's continual guidance. That guidance is neither dispensible or coercive. It is real and powerful, and it takes the form of an infinite dialect. For creation. (Dembski, 2009)

The argument here is that 'the effects of the rebellion of both humans and angels have—and continue to have consequences—consequences that appear to be synonymous with 'Natural Evil' (i.e. that evil is simply a consequence of the evolution of the biosphere—over 4.5 billion years or so of its history). This idea, *in faciem*, seems to be at odds with the very notion of a 'Benevolent Creator'. Theists that hold the view that God has set the 'whole thing going', naturally conclude that God is not involved in the 'everyday things'—indeed it seems as if 'the divine foot' is prohibited from entry. Those holding this view are likely to conclude that this world is not only the best possible world but the only possible world. It may be assumed furthermore that those holding a restrictive view of God's sovereignty, both from a theologically defined 'materialist' view, and an 'openness' theological perspective, may conclude that God, due to his lack of omnipotence, may not be held responsible for—at least natural evil.

It is, of course possible to view this world as the best of possible worlds but, I suggest, only in the light of it being the best of possible worlds for the ultimate purposes of God ; furthermore it makes no sense to describe this world as the only possible world that God could have created—and then advocate the idea of this same God being able to produce a 'New Heaven and New Earth'. It is worthwhile noting here the view held by C.S.Lewis, i.e. ' it is a false picture of providence that represents God and nature as being contained in a common time.' (Lewis, 1960) Lewis' comment is particularly salient for the twenty-first century enquirer or 'professor of faith' when philosophical notions of absolutes 'disalow' the likelyhood of God's 'omniscience' or 'omnipotence', Ergo God is neither omniscient or onnipotent—or anything else much.

Dembski makes the point that the God of Judeo/Christianity has always existed—and is the ultimate expression of 'personality' rather than an impersonal entity described as nothing more tangible than 'the ground of being'."God has acted on the basis of intentions and meanings. The world, by contrast, has a beginning and an end. It operates according to the 'causal-temporal' logic because, God, in an intentional act, created it that way. Divine action is, therefore, a more fundamental mode of causation. Intoxicated as it is with nature, our current mental environment resists this conclusion…" (Dembski, 2009)

Events Have Consequences

Does God possess comprehensive knowledge of what Dembski refers to as 'future contingent propositions'? The answer is an unequable yes. Of course. Theodicies that 'offer.' a model of divine limitation can absolve their particular 'deity'—even bring about a verdict of 'Not Guilty' but in so doing they malign the person of the God of Scripture, who is the ultimate expression of both power and goodness. Dembski suggests that—"to argue against God's ability to know future contingent propositions invariably involves questionable assumptions about the world, though created by God, might nonetheless impede God's knowledge of the future." It is the case that, because of a subliminally dominant view of the 'nature of reality', many are content with a lesser 'god'—a god who could not possibly, under any circumstances whatsoever, be allowed to 'put a divine foot in the door'. Moreover, the very idea that any kind of 'Fall from grace' could have allowed any kind of deity to produce the world, Dembski suggests, is merely anathema.

> Because God knows the future and can act on his knowledge by anticipating events and directing their course, divine action follows not a causal-temporal logic but an intentional-semantic logic. This logic treats time as nonlinear (Kairos) and sees God acting in the world to accomplish his purposes in accord with the meaning or

significance of events. The causal-temporal logic underlying the physical world and the intentional-semantic logic underlying divine action are not at odds. (Dembski, 2009)

The idea that God should inflict a system of parasitism, predation, pain and (premature) death (a system that has at its 'core' the merciless production of 'naturally selected' life-experiences—seemingly inflicted on innocent creatures) produces both consternation and disbelief. Such responses are because anything other than a naturalist explanation for the origin and sustenance of the biosphere will not suffice and do not fit with what we think we know about God's universe and God's ability to order it according to His designs and purposes. There is, as Dembski opines, a necessity to recognise that Genesis 1 describes God's original plan for creation, and moreover that Genesis 2&3 describe the man's placement within the Garden in Eden and the expulsion of both the man & woman from the garden—from the presence of God, i.e The Adamic Fall.

Dembski suggests that although it may be deduced that'The Fall 'subverted the plans and purposes of God'—whatever the effects there was 'no Post Fall—'radically new creative activity from God':

Evil is always parasitic, never creative. Indeed all our words for evil presupposes a good that has been subverted.

Impurity presupposes purity; unrighteousness presupposes righteousness, transgression presupposes a boundary that has been 'stepped across.' , and deviation presupposes a way from which we have departed. To see evil as parasitic is not to deny or trivialise it but rather to see it for what it is. Evil does not create; it only deforms. God's immediate response to the Fall is therefore not to create anew but to control the damage. (Dembski, 2009)

NB. God's ultimate response to the Fall is at the Cross—to undo the damage and then, at Christ's second coming, to create/reveal a new heaven and a new earth.

If, as Dembski suggests, evil cannot produce anything other than the subversion of 'the good' or the counterfeiting of the original then it would be expected that the attempts of Fallen Angels to disguise their acts of deviance within the created order would have failed miserably and would have, by the discerning eye, been seen as the works of evil—even that which is considered 'natural'.

He set another parable before them saying, "The Kingdom of the heavens has been likened to a man sowing good seed in his field. But, when men were asleep, his enemy came and sowed darnel-seeds as well, in among the grain, and departed. And when the crop sprouted and bore fruit the darnel-seeds also appeared." And the householder's slaves, approaching, said to him, "Lord, did you not so good seed in your field? Where have the darnel-seeds it contains come from?" And he said to them, "Someone who is an enemy did this." So the slaves say to him, "Do you wish then that we should go out and gather them?" But he says, "No, lest in the gathering of the darnel-seeds you should uproot the grain along with them. Let them grow up together until the harvest; and at the time of the harvest I shall tell the reapers," First gather the darnel-seeds and tie them in sheaves in order to burn them; but gather the grain into my granary." (Matthew 13:24-30) (Bentley Hart)

The (Chronos) moment that the pair in The Garden of Eden (in paradise) believed 'another voice', was the moment that God's judgement against rebellion was exacted. Ironically, it was not just the 'beginning' (Kairos) of a world in which evil of all kinds appears to hold sway but 'the beginning' of the redemptive process that would hail God's victory over sin and death. Moreover, this 'Chronos moment' of rebellion by 'Adamah' was, possibly, the 'moment' when the Fallen Angels realized that they had also been found wanting and, were also, to be expelled from the paradise of God.

If, as William Dembski suggests, this 'space-time' act of rebellion by the progenitors of humankind was that which brought about the kairological subjugation of creation; it is, I suggest, the case that the 'space-time' misjudgment on the part of extra-terrestrials, i.e. the failure of these 'sons of God' to fully comprehend the value, plans and purposes the creator had in mind for humankind—was that which not only preceded the Genesis Fall in chronological time but that superseded it in terms of its ramifications for the 'Very Good' Creation of God. "<u>And God saw everything that he had made, and behold it was very good</u>." (Genesis 1:31). In other words, the ability of these 'agents of God's will' to bring about a less than desirous state of affairs within the biosphere is, I suggest, a strong possibility—a state of affairs that brings about more than 'necessary' harms within creation that would otherwise be anticipated within an evolutionary process. These 'august creatures'—these 'fallen angels' had failed to fully comprehend the sovereignty of God. Indeed, these space-time moments of destiny when the immorality of both men and angels was written across the heavens—the moment when God subjugated all of creation to that which Christ alone could release from its bondage to decay and death.

Dembski's argument is that 'God creates in God's time (Kairos) then implements this first creation as a second creation in time (Chronos). In other words: at the 'moment' of human rebellion (though the Angelic rebellion had occurred 'previously' *[see above]*—God acts[63] to restore the second creation NB .a 'creation/re-creation'—to be revealed at the Eschaton). Moreover,

---

[63]Genesis to Revelation is the story of God's pursuit of fallen humanity; it is a relentless pursuit that required the ultimate sacrifice from God and a 'heart' response from humankind: "Do you love me...?" Is the question.

because God is unfettered by time, God can bring about the restoration of the original creation. Furthermore, by acting across time, God responds to the Adamic Fall by working, not merely after the event but before it.

Dembski's suggestion, i.e. that we accept that God acts (Kairologically) to anticipate the Fall of Adam (Genesis 3) has much merit because it removes the need to prioritize 'the age of the biosphere' as a defining part of one's theological conclusions. Here I am in agreement with Dembski but would also add that God possesses foreknowledge of every conceivable event including the Angelic Fall. Ergo God acts 'in anticipation of this event also'.

Dembski makes good use of God's sovereignty as displayed in God's active, providential and permissive will:

> Active—what God does when God brings about certain states of affairs. Providential—when God orders the creation giving it a 'determinate' character so that it consistently displays the patterns and movements for which it was designed. God's Permissive Will is that which allows for specific events and the consequences of these events.

Dembski gives an example of God permitting Satan to have control over the life of Job. Another example would be that of the life of Joseph (Genesis chapters 37-50) All three forms of God's will are seen to be involved in the disordering of creation: Genesis 3:17,18 ('cursed is the ground'). Moreover, Paul's confirmation of

God's active will as God brings about the subjugation of the creation.

Ostensibly (*in faciem*) there seems to be little difference between God's 'foreknowledge' of events, which allows God to act in bringing about the best of possible outcomes, and the notion of God's acting in Kairos Time, apart from the possible confusion arising from the notion of 'Middle Knowledge.', i.e. that God has knowledge of all events across space/time but, possibly, no control over such 'events', i.e. the unknown/unknowable actions of free-will-agents.

Dembski's view: That because of God's 'Kairos' knowledge of the Adamic Fall, God brought about the creative 'Status Quo'—a state of affairs that has, physically, existed since 'The Beginning' of the biosphere, as punishment for the deviancy of the progenitors of humankind—is feasible but not at all necessary. My view is that there is no need to 'apportion' blame to 'Adam & Eve' as it was the 'pre-creational rebellion' of angels that we can say is responsible for 'the nature of things'--ironically for the creation of 'the best possible world'—a world that would enable the redemption of God's 'very Good' creation through the, life,death and resurrection of the second person of the Trinity. Moreover,before' the creation of the universe—in an entirely different 'environment'— an environment/ dimension/ *reality in which there 'is' no question over God's omniscience:* God had foreknowledge of the action of these angels and (consequently) the 'potentiality for the corruption that these 'agents of creation' brought about in the biosphere. Moreover, the subjugation that the apostle Paul refers to in Romans 8:19-25 is not, necessarily, that which the creation has experienced since its genesis, but may be considered something other, i.e. the removal of the pair from the presence of God (from the tree of life) resulting in death (Genesis 2:15-17, 3:23):

The increase in their experience of pain (Genesis **3:16). NB. *They must have been aware of the 'experience of pain'** because of their physiology and so would have been cognizant of the consequences that disobedience would bring about—though they might not have fully understood the implications regarding their descendants.* We may assume that they had no thought of any such outcomes.

And God saw everything that [HE] had made, and behold, it was very good.(Genesis 1:31)

The Future, Our Future

We listen with a thrill and a shudder as our scientists and philosophers speculate on these subjects. Nearly always they speak of the future of the physical cosmos, and possibly of the human race as well. But they may have no 'personal' hope for such a future (of the individual)—not so much as to discuss something so inanely metaphysical. And yet, such people hold tenaciously to a future for the cosmos—or for the renewal of the biosphere. Even those who say the Universe 'popped' into existence out of nothing may not like to consider that (as luck or the laws of physics would have it) it may pop out of existence'—even prior to its 'saving'— and its 'saving' would, most likely, have been unnecessary should humankind have not: 'known better than God', have 'gone their own way', or have 'realized' their responsibilities as 'stewards' of this amazing world.

'When Christ, who is your life, shall appear', Paul says, 'then you too will be revealed with him as glorious' (Colossians 3:4). And, 'How great a love the Father has lavished on upon us,' John exclaims, 'that we should be described as children of God! But it has not yet been shown what we shall be. We only know that when he appears we shall be as he is' (1 John 3:1-2). Reverting to Paul, 'He will transform our lowly body to be like his glorious body, using the powers he has over everything' (Philippians 3:20) Dallas Willard 'The Divine Conspiracy'

Summary

Throughout the duration of this book I have sought to establish whether or not it was possible to successfully argue that the God of biblical theism, being identified as the master craftsman of the creation of the physical universe, could possibly be the architect, creator/sustainer of life throughout a so-called [Darwinian evolutionary] history of the biosphere. And I concluded that it is entirely plausible to find that the God of Christian Scriptures, who is both omnipotent and benevolent, ordained the known physical laws (laws that allow for a world in which suffering and death prevail) to bring about the best of possible outcomes. I reasoned that the creation should be considered 'good'—even 'very good' as opposed to 'perfect'.

I proposed that it was after the creation of the imago Deo, that creation was pronounced 'very good'—moreover that there is sufficient reason to refute the notion of the creation being perfect at its inception.

I developed an argument for both the existence of angels and for the rebellion of the so-called 'Fallen Angels' i.e. extraterrestrial intelligence—an intelligence that continues to offer opposition to all that God has intended for his creation—especially the redemption of mankind. I concluded that because of the '

Angelic Fall there was, propositionally, some kind of distortion in the functioning of physical laws—a distortion that would produce outcomes that may be considered less than perfect. Indeed, I argued that this does not preclude the possibility of there being 'interferences' within the biosphere (within an evolutionary synthesis)—interferences that may have allowed for states of affairs that (while allowing for the flourishing of lower life forms) allowed for an increase in the suffering (especially but not exclusively) of higher-order-sentient life.

I argued that in spite of the difficulty in advocating God's goodness within an evolutionary framework the implications do not present an insurmountable hurdle to the work of evolutionary defence/theodicy.

I considered the ingenuity of philosophical theologians—in their attempt to offer an alternative for the God of Scripture and argued that even though their efforts are creative—at least in terms of an alternative view of the deity—they are not relevant to any defence that takes the traditional views of God's character seriously. Moreover, I reasoned that the 'Ground of Being' (aka 'the universe') alternative along with other philosophical theologies are not at all convincing—and are an unnecessary deviancy from the traditional view God as a [Triune] personality: 'A Determinate Entity'. Indeed, many such views offer an alternative 'god' rather than offering an argument for the Benevolence of the God of the Bible. I interacted with various defences/theodicies, that in the light of the so-called 'Modern Evolutionary Synthesis' have offered differing perspectives ending with an up-to-date review of the theodicies of Irenaeus and Augustine.

In conclusion, I argued that, at a particular juncture in (chronological) time, the second person of the Trinity became a man so that He, and only He, could, through his death and resurrection, defeat the evil brought about by the rebellion of men and angels—thus making possible a way back from 'Eden' for mankind—from alienation into the presence of God on the New Earth.

Mine is a 'Free-Will Defence' of both 'Men & Angels'

Derek J. White

May 2019

Works Cited

A., P., 2011. *Where The Conflict Really Lies.* New York: OUP.

Alexander, D., 2008. *Creation or Evolution: Do We Have to Choose?.* Oxford: Monarch.

Alexander, D. R., 2018. *Is There Purpose In Biology.* Oxford: Lion.

Alter, R., 1997. *Genesis: Translation and Commentary.* New York & London: W.W. Norton.

Andrews, E., 2018. *What is Man? Adam,Alien or Ape?*. Nashville: Elm Hill.

Aquinas, T., 2003. *on Evil.* Oxford: OUP.

Astley, J., 2009. Evolution and Evil:The Difference Darwinism Makes in Theology and Spirituality. In: D. &. W. S. Barton, ed. *Reading Genesis after Darwin.* Oxford: OUP.

Bauckham, R., 1999. *God will be all in alll:The Eschatology of Jurgen Moltmann.* Edinburgh: T&T Clark.

Behe, M., 2007. *The Edge of Evolution.* New York: Free Press.

Bentley Hart, D., 2013. *The Experience of God:Being,Consciousness,Bliss.* New Haven & London: Yale University Press.

Bentley Hart, D., 2017. *The New Testament.* Yale: Yale University Press.

Bimson, J., 2006. Reconsidering the Cosmic Fall. *Science and Christian Belief,* Volume 18, pp. 63-81.

Bird, M.F. Evans, C.A. Gathercole, S.J. Hill, C.E. Tilling,C, 2014. *How God Became Jesus: The Real Origins of Belief in Jesus' Divine Nature.* Grand Rapids: Zondervan.

Blocher, H., 1994. *Evil and the Cross.* Leicester: Apollos.

Boyd, G., 1997. *God at War:The Bible & Spiritual Conflict.* Downers Grove: IVP Academic.

Boyd, G., 2001. *Satan and the Problem of Evil.* Downers Grove: IVP.

Bruce, F., 1960. *The New Testament Documents: Are they Reliable?.* 6 ed. Leicester: IVP.

Carroll, W., 2000. "Creation,Evolution, and Thomas Aquinas". *Revue des Questions Scientifiques 4*, pp. 319-347.

Casas, David., 2016. Adam And The Image Of God. In: *Searching for Adam:Genesis & the Truth About Man's Origins.* s.l.:Masters Books.

Cassuto, U., 1998. *Commentary on the Book of Genesis:Part 1, From Adam to Noah.* Jerusalem: The Magnus Press (The Hebrew University).

Clayton, P. &. K. S., 2007. Divine Action and The Argument from Neglect. In: N. R. R. S. W. Murphy, ed. *Physics & Cosmology (Scientific Perspectives on the Problem of Natural Evil).* Vatican City: Vatican Observatory Publications, pp. 179-180.

Cobb, J. &. G. D., 1976. *Process Theology.* Louisville: John Knox Press.

Collins, C., 2011. *Did Adam and Eve Really Exist? (who were they and why it matters).* Nottingham: IVP.

Collins, C. J., 2006. *Genesis 1-4.* Phillipsburg: P&R.

Conway Morris, S., 2003. *Life's Solutions: Inevitable Humans in a Lonely Universe.* Cambridge: CUP.

Copan, P. &. L. C. W., 2004. *Creation out of Nothing: A Biblical, Philosophical, and Scientific Exploration.* Leicester: Apollos.

Davidson, I., 2011. God of Salvation:Sociology in Theological Perspective. In: I. &. R. M. Davidson, ed. *God of Salvation:Sociology in Theological Perspective.* Farnham: Ashgate.

Davis, S., 2001. Free Will and Evil. In: S. Davis, ed. *Encountering Evil.* Edinburgh: T&T Clark, p. 6.

Dawkins, R., 1996. *River out of Eden: A darwinian View of Life.* London: Phe

Dembski, W. A., 2009. *The End of Christianity: Finding a Good God in an Evil World.* Nashville: B&H Publishing House.

Dennett, D., 2003. *Freedom Evolves.* London: Penguin Group.

Doyle, R., 1999. *Eschatology and the Shape of Christian Belief.* Carlisle: Paternoster.

Dunn, J., 2003. *The Theology of Paul the Apostle.* London: T&T Clark.

Dye, C., 2013. *Colin Dye.* [Online]
Available at: http://www.colindye.com/2013/02/06/the-victory-of-the-cross/
[Accessed 13 July 2014].

Ehrman, B., 2014. *How Jesus Became God: The Exultation of a Jewish Preacher from Galilee.* New York: Harper One.

Ewart, P., 2009. The Necessity of Chance:Randomness,Purpose and the Sovereignty of God. *Science and Christian Belief,* Issue October 2009, pp. 111-129.

Frankl, V., 1988. *The Will to Meaning:Foundations and Applications of Logotherapy.* New York: Penguin Books.

Gathercole, S., 2006. *The Pre-existent Son:Recovering the Christologies of Matthew, Mark and Luke.* Grand Rapids: Eerdmans.

Goldberg, L., 2009. *God, Torah, Messiah:The Messianic Jewish Theology.* San Fransico: Purple Pomegranite.

Green, Joel B., 2017. "Adam, What Have You Done?" New Testament Voices on the Origins of Sin. In: *Evolution And The Fall.* Grand Rapids: Eerdmans.

Grenshaw, J., 2005. *Defending God: Biblical Responses to the Problem of Evil.* Oxford: OUP.

Griffin, D., 2001. *Reenchantment without Supernaturalism.* New York: Cornell University Press.

Griffin, L. &., 1996. *Jewish Theology and Process Thought.* New York: NYSU.

Groothius, D., 2000. *Truth Decay.* s.l.:s.n.

Harari, Y., 2014. *Sapiens: A Brief History of Mankind.* London: Random House (Penguin).

Haught, J., 2001. *God After Darwin:A Theology of Evolution.* Boulder: West View Press.

Haught, J., 2010. *Making Sence of Evolution:Darwin, God, and the Drama of Life.* Louiaville: WJK.

Hayward, A., 1985. *Creation and Evolution: The Facts and the Fallacies.* London: SPCK.

Heiser, M. S., 2015. *The Unseen Realm: Recovering the Supernatural Worldview of the Bible.* Bellingham(WA): Lexham Press.

Hendriksen, W., 1980. *New Testament Commentary: Romans 1-8.* Edinburgh: Banner of Truth Trust.

Herzog, W., 2000. *Jesus, Justice and The Reign of God.* Louisville, Kentucky: Westminster John Knox Press.

Hick, J., 2010. *Evil and the God of Love.* 10th ed. London: Palgrove Macmillan.

Hough, A., 2010. *The Flaw in the Universe: Natural Disaster and Human Sin.* Winchester: O-Books.

Hurtado, L., 2005. *How on Earth did Jesus become a God?: Historical Questions about Earliest Devotion to Jesus.* Grand Rapids/Cambridge: Eerdmans.

Hutchinson, I., 2011. *Monopolizing Knowledge:a scientist refutes religion-denying, reason-destroying scientism.* Belmont, Massachusetts: Fias Publishing.

Israel, M., 1995. *Angels: Messengers of Grace.* London: SPCK.

Johnson, D., 2001. *Triumph of the Lamb: A Commentary on Revelation.* Phillipaburg: P&R Publishing.

Johnstone, D., 2009. *davidjohnstone.net/blogs.* [Online].

König, A., 1989. *The Eclipse of Christ in Eschatology: Toward a Christ-Centered Approach.* London: Eardmans.

Kreeft, P., 1995. *Angels (and Demons): What do we really know about them?.* San Francisco: Inatius Press.

Lamoureux, D., 2013. No Historical Adam:Evolutionary Creation View. In: M. &. C. Barrett, ed. *Four Views on the Historical Adam.* Grand Rapids: Zondervan.

Leibniz, G., 2001. Theodicy. In: M. Larrimore, ed. *The Problem of Evil.* Oxford: Blackwell, p. 197.

Lennox, J., 2011. *Seven Days that Divide the World: The Beginning According to Genesis and Science.* Grand Rapids: Zondervan.

Leslie, J., 1989. *Universes.* London & New York: Routledge.

Lewis, C., 1960. *The Problem of Pain.* San Francisco: HarperCollins.

Lewis, C., 1996. *The Problem of Pain.* San Francisco: Harper.

Linzey, A., 2000. God News for the World?. *Third Way,* June.pp. 23-25.

Lloyd, M., 1998. Are Animals Fallen. In: D. &. Y. Linzey, ed. *Animals on the Agenda.* London: SCM.

Lloyd, M., 2018. Theodicy,Fall, and Adam. In: S. P. Rosenberg , ed. *iFnding Ourselves After Darwin.* Grand Rapids: Baker Academic.

Losos, j., 2017. *Improbable Destinies:How Predictable is Evolution?.* UK: Penguin Random House.

Lowman, P., 2002. *A Long Way East of Eden.* Carlisle: Paternoister.

Lucas, E., 2001. *Can We Believe Genesis Today?.* Leicester: IVP.

Mauser, U., 1991. One God Alone: A Pillar of Biblical Theology. *The Princton Seminary Bulletin,* pp. 255-265.

McCabe, H., 2010. *Good AND Evil: In The Theology of St Thomas Aquinas.* London & New York: Continuum.

McCord Adams, M., 1999. *Horrendous Evils and the Goodness of God.* New York: Cornell University Press.

McGrath, A., 1993. *Evangelicalism and the Future of Christianity.* London: Hodder & Stoughton.

McGrath, A., 2011. *Darwinism and the Divine.* Chichester: Blackwell.

Meeks, D. M., 2006. *The Social Trinity and Property.* Minneapolis: Fortress Press.

Messer, N., 2009. *(Theology after Darwin).* Milton Keynes: Paternoister.

Messer, N., 2007. *Selfish Genes & Christian Ethics.* London: SCM.

Middleton, J., 2005. *The Liberating Image: The Imago Dei in Genesis 1.* Grand Rapids: Brazos Press.

Middleton, R., 2014. *A New Heaven and a New Earth:Reclaiming Biblical Eschatology.* Grand Rapids: Baker Academic.

Mitchell. C.Ben, 2018. Questions,Challenges, and Concerns for the Problem of Evil. In: *Finding Ourselves After Darwin.* Grand Rapids: Baker Academic.

Moltmann, J., 1993. *The Crucified God: Foundations and Criticism of Christian Theology.* s.l.:Fortress.

Moltmann, J., 1996. *The Coming of God.* London: SCM Press.

Moreland, J., 2009. *The Recalcitrant Imago Dei:Human Persons and the Failure of Naturalism.* London: SCM Press.

Morris, L., 1998. *The Epistle to the Romans.* Grand Rapids: Eerdmans.

Murray, M. J., 2008. *Nature Red in Tooth & Claw.* 2011 ed. Oxford & New York: OUP.

Nicholi, A., 2002. *The Question of God: C.S. Lewis And Sigmund Freud Debate God,Love,Sex And The Meaning Of Life.* New York: Free Press.

Osborn, R., 2014. *Death Before the Fall.* Downers Grove USA: IVP Academic.

Osborn, R., 2014. *Death Before The Fall.* Downers Grove: IVP Academic.

Penelhum, T., 1990. Divine Goodness and the Problem of Evil. In: M. McCord-Adams. M. Adams, ed. *The Problem of Evil.* Oxford: OUP.

Perry, M., 2015. *Evolution2.* Dallas exas): Benbella Books Inc.

Plantinga, A., 1974. *God,Freedom and Evil.* Grand Rapids: Erdmans.

Plantinga, A., 2011. *Where the Conflict Really Lies: Science,Religion,& Naturalism.* Oxford & New York: OUP.

Polkinghorne, J., 1986. *One World: the interaction of science and theology.* London: SPCK.

Polkinghorne, J., 1991. *Reason & Reality.* London: SPCK.

Polkinghorne, J., 2002. *The God of Hope and the End of the World.* London: SPCK.

Riches, A., 2017. The Mystery of Adam: A Poetic Apology for the Traditional Doctrine. In: *Evolution And The Fall.* Grand Rapids: Eerdmans, p. 124.

Robinson, A. & Southgate, C., 2011. Theology and Evolutionary Biology. In: C. Southgate, ed. *God,Humanity and the Cosmos.* 3rd, ed. s.l.:T&T Clark.

Ross, A., 1988. *Creation and Blessing:A Guide to the Study and Exposition of the Book of Genesis.* Grand Rapids: Baker Books.

Russell, R., 2008. Natural Theodicy in an Evolutionary Context: The Need for an Eschatology of New Creation. In: *Cssmology: From Alpha to Omega.* Minneapolis: Fortress Press, pp. 249-272.

Russell, R. J., 2008. *Cosmology: From Alpha to Omega.* Minneapolis: Fortress Press.

Sailhamer, J., 2011. *Genesis Unbound: A Provocative New Look at the Creation Account.* 2nd. ed. USA: BookVillages.

Sanlon, P., 2014. *Simply God: Recovering The Classical Trinity.* Nottingham: IVP.

Shore, J., 2005. *Penguins,Pain and the Whole Shebang.* New York: Seabury Books.

Southgate, C., 2008. *The Groaning of Creation.* Louisiville: Westminster John Knox Press.

Stackhouse, J., 1998. *Can God Be Trusted?: Faith and the Challenge of Evil.* Oxford: OUP.

Stoeger, W., 2007. Entropy,Emergence, and the Physical Roots of Natural Evil. In: N. Murphy & R. Russell, eds. *Physics and Cosmology:Scientific Perspectives on the Problem of Natural Evil.* Vatican City State: Vatican Observatory Publications.

Storms, S., 2013. *Kingdom Come:The Amillennial Alternative.* Fearn, Ross-shire: Mentor.

Storms, S., 2018. *10 Things you should know about the Imago Dei.* [Online] Available at: www.samstorms.com
[Accessed 11 May 2019].

Stump, E., 2012. *Wandering in Darkness: Narrative and the Problem of Suffering.* Oxford: OUP.

Swinburne, R., 1997. *The Evolution of the Soul: Revised Edition.* Oxford: OUP.

Swinburne, R., 1998. *Providence and the Problem of Evil.* London: Clarendon Press.

Swinton, J., 2007. *Raging with Compassion:Pastoral Responses to the Problem of Evil.* Grand Rapids: Eerdmans.

Tiegreen, C., 2006. *Why a Suffering World Makes Sense.* Grand Rapids: Baker Books.

Tinker, M., 2010. *Reclaiming Genesis.* Oxford: Monarch.

Trotter, A., 1997. *Interpreting the Epistle to the Hebrews.* Grand Rapids: Baker Books.

Turl, J., 2010. Substance Dualism or Body-Soul Duality. *Science and Christian Belief,* April, 22(1), pp. 57-80.

Turner, J. S., 2017. *Purpose & Desire:What Makes Something "Alive" And Why Modern Darwinism Has failed To Explain It.* New York: Harper Collins.

Vardy, P., 1992. *The Puzzle of Evil.* Glasgow: Fount.

Waltke, B., 2001. *Genesis: A Commentary.* Grand Rapids: Zondervan.

Walton, J., 2009. *The Lost World of Genesis One.* Downers Grove : IVP Acadamic.

Ward, K., 1990. *Divine Action:Examining God's Role in an Open and Emergent Universe.* London: Collins.

Ward, K., 2008. *Why There Almost Certainly Is a God.* Oxford: Lion.

Webb, S., 2010. *The Dome of Eden:A New Solution to the Problem of Creation and Evolution.* Eugene: Cascade Books.

Wenham, G., 1987. *Genesis 1-15 (Word Biblical Commentary.* Waco: Word Books.

Wildman, W., 2011. 'Narnia's Aslan,Earth's Darwin and Heaven's God'. *DIALOGUE [a journal of Mormon thought],* 44(No2/Summer 2011).

Wilkinson, D., 2009. Worshiping The Creator. In: R. &. N. T. Berry, ed. *Darwin Creation and the Fall.* Nottingham: Apollos.

Williams, P., 2002. *The Case for Angels.* Carlisle: Paternoster Press.

Williams, R., 2000. *On Christian Theology.* Oxford: Blackwell.

Williams, T., 2013. *Anselm,Saint.* [Online]
Available at:
<http://plato.stanford.edu/archives/spr2013/entries/anselm/>
[Accessed 12 April 2014].

Wilson, J., 2013. *God's Good World: Reclaiming the Doctrine of Creation.* Grand Rapids: Baker Academic.

Wright, N., 1992. *The New Testament and the People of God.* London: SPCK.

Wright, N., 2003. *The Resurrection of the Son of God.* London: SPCK.

Wright, N., 2006. *Evil and the Justice of God.* London: SPCK.

Wright, N., 2006. Evil and the Justice of God.

Yamauchi, E., 2003. In: B. H. W. R. Archer, ed. *Theological Workbook of the Old Testament.* Chicago: Moody.

APPENDIX

Thinking 'Allowed' On 'World Views'

Atheism & Absolutes

By 'atheism' I mean: a view that, in particular, denies the existence of the God of the Judeo/Christian Scriptures—a view that disallows the possibility of the existence of anything other than the 'material' or the 'illusion of the material'. These may include ideas that view the universe and all 'within' (Panpsychism) as the 'mother of all inventions' i.e. that which produces all that exists or has ever existed in the physical universe or 'Evolutionism'—that which adheres to the view that the universe/the biosphere are nothing but the product of blind chance i.e. 'Natural Selection'. 'Evolutionism' (not to be confused with Theistic-Evolution) is the denial of anything that may intrude into the story of 'life's existence'—whether fairies or goblins or anything that does not fit into the material paradigm. Panpsychism is the view that claims that all of 'matter' throughout the universe is, in some way (individually) conscious and yet is 'One' (Monism).

The universe is, de facto, 'self-regenerating'; it is what it is—without beginning…

Atheists may have their own list of absolutes—their own 'list of taboos', i.e. absolute standards of 'right & wrong'. Any such standards are usually a part of a 'collective conscience' from their particular culture—or may have been standards that have been imposed on society by a dictatorial regime or simply have evolved through 'Natural Selection'—the whim of Social Mores. Of course, it is the case that any such conventions may bring order rather than chaos within any such society. It would, of course, be difficult to maintain such 'ideals' without 'the rule of law'. And even if such a list were policed by that law they would only pertain to any given society—regimes, nations or even empires; they are seldom 'universal' in their effect; what is acceptable within a particular society may not be acceptable in another, e.g. Islamic (Sharia) Law would not, usually, be acceptable in a country with a strong Christian Heritage.

The implications are obvious. Take for example the Ten Commandments (believed to have been given by the creator and sustainer of the universe to a group of disenfranchised nomads: Exodus 20:1-21). The list is well known in our own society as the laws of the country have been, mostly, derived from them. These commandments were given as 'Absolutes'.

If there were no belief in the divine origin to these commandments or disbelief in their authority or validity it would make little difference to their 'Absolute Nature'. Of course, any given society may wish to disregard them but that would be to that society's detriment. If any member of a society with such agreed conventions were to decide to break one of its own 'self-generated' commandments, there may be consequences (some worse than others) but these consequences would not be universal or eternal.

Atheists have no grounds for belief in standards that are anything other than temporal. Any such beliefs are, indeed, transient.

Islam:

For Muslims, Allah is 'The Almighty' and, even 'The Merciful' yet evil exists and no explanation is given apart from: 'God is (always) Great! In the Quran, there is no real mention of an Adamic Fall[64] from grace. The way Allah deals with human failure is to measure the pass rate for the five pillars[65] [duties] and to

---

[64] The Quran says: "..but approach not this tree, or you will run into harm and transgression." [The Heifer 35]. Nowhere is there any mention of 'original sin' although there are 'numerous' references to Hell and Judgement.

[65] The Quran lists five pillars [duties] that Muslims have to comply with: profession of faith, prayer, giving to charity, fasting during Ramadan [a month during the year when Muslims fast between sunrise and sunset] and making a pilgrimage [Hajj] to Mecca. There are some variations according to differing traditional statements [Hadiths] that are not in the actual Quran.

weigh the good and the not so good on the divine scales. These are the scales that decide the eternal fate of the individual. Heaven or Hell is down to the individual's efforts to, if possible, put things right. Ultimately, Muslims cannot know the 'final outcome' until the day of judgement when Allah will decide how their lives 'match up' to Allah's expectations. Allah, it seems, does not deal with the problem of sin and evil. Moreover, there does not appear to be any sense of grace within the Islamic tradition—at least not in the form of 'undeserved favor'—though there are, according to some Quranic traditions, ways in which the adherent may enter the 'perfect state of wellbeing'.

Buddhism:

For Buddhists, there is no such thing as the 'human problem'—at least concerning the notion of a creator [God] because the very idea of GOD ('god') is anathema to adherents of Monism. The only 'problem' Buddhist philosophy has is with the individual 'self'— just being 'you' is 'bad news'. The 'self' is the problem, so the objective of this World View is to become 'selfless'—to reach a point where the 'not-self' has, somehow—in spite of the effort— reached the ideal and has managed to fulfil its obligation[66] so that it

---

[66] In Buddhist philosophy the self (however one describes self in the endless cycle of 're-birth') is in debt to an unidentifiable source (not deity). In order appease the source—to cease being 'self' (personality, which is a socially constructed phenomena)—the individual has without personal effort) to reach the ultimate state of existence' to cease 'existence' and, therefore, become nothing.

270

[the not-self] can 'achieve' Nirvana. The Buddha 's, philosophical, view holds that we are 'all' a part of 'the one'—the personal 'we' should cease to exist for the individual self is nothing but part of the one: a drop in the bucket of a greater 'ultimate meaning'[67]. For Buddhist philosophy, the problem of suffering has nothing whatsoever to do with human rebellion against a Creator. Generally, Buddhist philosophy offers no substantial account for any kind of god/deity; though it may be said that Buddhist philosophy has everything to do with human desire—the ultimate 'goal' being to escape from 'the desire to desire'.Buddhists in general (not all, of course) are considered to be—at least potentially—'desirous' (my word not theirs) to leave this vale of tears and so to emasculate themselves into 'the grand nothingness'. The problem of evil is in the very nature of 'being'—whatever form of carbon-based life that may be[68]. The irony with monistic views of reality is that any moral compass that adherents might wish to live by cannot be justified from monism but mus, on the contrary, be interpreted in the light of a 'Universal Moral Code' that just so 'happens' to be in existence in spite of the impersonal nature of monistic ideas.. However, the notion of justice is circular, it goes round and round and gets

---

[67] Rick Richardson. 'Spirituality:what does it mean to be spiritual?' IVP

[68] The Buddha (Gautama), being from a Hindu culture, had a similar idea of reality. For Hindus (generally) God is everything and everything is God, which means that we are 'God' [Brahman] and the soul [Atman] is also 'God'—they are the same— we are all, ultimately, the same—'We' Are God. The question of who 'God' is then, I suggest, rather non sequitur.

nowhere; no one individual will be held responsible as the ultimate goal of Buddhist philosophy is to escape personality—there will be no 'one' individual as all will be one with the one—all will dissipate into nothing in particular—so to speak. "Bad karma is like a wheel that will either crush you or enable 'you' to break free from the repetition, i.e. when 'you' have lived a pure life." [69]

The point here is not to stand in judgement over other people's opinions or 'world views' but to offer something that helps the reader connect with the overall subject of this book: The purposes of God for creation'. Indeed, it is the inherent right of any, individual to hold whatever beliefs they wish—or are so constrained to believe by their social mores. Of course, just as others may 'judge' God, so God should be allowed the privilege of making a judgement on His creatures—whether or not it is God's right to do so. Of course, the issue being addressed in this book is the converse; here I am addressing the question of God's right to be considered anything other than a cosmic sadist, an impotent deity, or a figment of the imagination of latter-day products of blind chance.

---

[69] The Lotus and The Cross' [Ravi Zacharias]

ABOUT THE AUTHOR

Derek has been married to Jackie since September 1963. Derek & Jackie have four [grown] children, eleven grandchildren—and two great grandchildren—exponential growth. Four of the grandkids live, with 'their parents', in Australia—proper Aussies.

Derek became a committed follower of Jesus Christ in 1976, previously having had 'strong leftish/ atheistic tendencies'. He has been in Christian leadership in various positions: An elder (eleven years) at Bournemouth Community Church with oversight for mission & apologetics; a deacon at Lansdowne [Baptist] Church Bournemouth (nine years) --working with international students and co-leading the Young People's Work [then YPF] with his wife Jackie. He was one of the founder directors of the International Training Network, Bournemouth: a training center for the teaching of English as a foreign language. Derek was the principal/director [1996-2010] of the Christian English Language Centre in Bournemouth and Christchurch, England. Since December 2014 Derek & Jackie have been attending St Mary's Church Ferndown, where they are seeking to use our gifts for the Mission of Christ.

Derek's 'academic' background includes forays into the world of: Sociology, Philosophical Theology, Philosophy & Apologetics, English-Language Pedagogy, Psycho-Linguistics at:

The Open University, The University of Sheffield, Canterbury Christchurch University, Trinity College, Newburgh USA, and The University of Exeter.

Soli Deo Gloria